DEPARTMENT OF THE NAVY
HEADQUARTERS UNITED STATES MARINE CORPS
3000 MARINE CORPS PENTAGON
WASHINGTON, DC 20350-3000

MCO P8020.10B
SD TBD
31 OCT 2007

MARINE CORPS ORDER P8020.10B

From: Commandant of the Marine Corps
To: Distribution List

Subj: MARINE CORPS AMMUNITION AND EXPLOSIVES SAFETY PROGRAM
        (Short Title: MARCORPSAMMOANDEXPLSAFETYPRO)

Ref: (a) OPNAVINST 8020.14/MCO P8020.11
        (b) DOD 6055.9-STD, "DOD Ammunition and Explosives
            Safety Standards," October 5, 2004
        (c) OPNAVINST 5102.1D/MCO P5102.1B
        (d) NAVSEA OP 5, Vol. 1 (NOTAL)
        (e) NOSSAINST 8023.11 (NOTAL)
        (f) MCO 8023.3A
        (g) NOSSAINST 8020.14 (NOTAL)
        (h) SECNAV M-5210.1
        (i) NAVMCDIR 5210.11E
        (j) NAVSEA OP 5, Vol. 3 (NOTAL)
        (k) MCO P5090.2A
        (l) DOD 4500.9-R, "Defense Transportation Regulation
            (DTR), Part II, Cargo Movement," November 2004
        (m) Title 49, Code of Federal Regulations (CFR),
            Parts 100-199, "Research and Special Programs
            Administration," Department of Transportation,
            current edition
        (n) BOE-6000-E, Bureau of Explosives (BOE) Tariff
            Service, Hazardous Materials Regulations of the
            Department of Transportation (NOTAL)
        (o) NAVSEA SW020-AC-SAF-010 (NOTAL)
        (p) NAVSEA SW020-AF-HBK-010 (NOTAL)
        (q) OPNAVINST 5530.13D/MCO P5530.14
        (r) DOD 5100.76-M, "Physical Security of Sensitive
            Conventional Arms, Ammunition, and Explosives,"
            August 12, 2000
        (s) NAVSEA SW023-AG-WHM-010 (NOTAL)
        (t) NAVSEA SW020-AG-SAF-010 (NOTAL)
        (u) MCO P4030.19H
        (v) NAVSEA OP 4 (NOTAL)
        (w) NAVFAC P-300

DISTRIBUTION STATEMENT A: Approved for public release;
distribution is unlimited.

(x) NAVSEA OP 3565, Volume 2 (NOTAL)
(y) MCO P4400.150E
(z) TM 11240-15/3D (NOTAL)
(aa) NAVSEA SW023-AH-WHM-010 (NOTAL)
(ab) MCO 3570.1B
(ac) NAVSEAINST 8020.7C (NOTAL)
(ad) MCO P1000.6G
(ae) MCO 3571.2F
(af) Marine Corps Bulletin 8011 (canc: Oct 07)
(ag) NAVAIR 00-80T-103 (NOTAL)
(ah) Title 40, Code of Federal Regulations (CFR), Part
     266, Subpart M, "Military Munitions"
(ai) SECNAV M-5214.1
(aj) NAVSUP P-724 (NOTAL)
(ak) OPNAVINST 8020.15/MCO 8020.13
(al) MCO 4450.12
(am) DOD 4160.21-M, "Defense Materiel Disposition
     Manual," August 18, 1997
(an) MCO 8025.1D
(ao) OPNAVINST 8000.16C
(ap) MCO 5100.29A
(aq) NAVSUP P-805/807 (NOTAL)
(ar) MIL-HDBK-274 (NOTAL)
(as) MCO 3500.27B
(at) Commander's Reference Guide, Land Mine and
     Explosives Hazards (Iraq) 13 Feb 2003 (NOTAL)

Encl: (1) Marine Corps Ammunition and Explosives Safety
           Directive

Report Requirement: List, page i

1. Situation. This Order provides policy for the
implementation, guidance, and oversight of the Marine Corps
Ammunition and Explosives Safety Program, and identifies
specific command responsibilities as they apply to the Program.

2. Cancellation. MCO P8020.10A.

3. Mission. To establish and execute the Marine Corps
ammunition and explosives safety policy for Class V materiel in
accordance with reference (a).

4. Execution

a. Commander's Intent and Concept of Operations

    (1) Commander's Intent. It is the intent of this Order to provide policy on the following:

        (a) Marine Corps Ammunition and Explosives Safety Program.
        (b) Interaction of the Marine Corps Ammunition and Explosives Safety Program and affected organizations.

    (2) Concept of Operations

        (a) The Secretary of Defense (SECDEF) has established basic explosives safety policies to be observed by Department of Defense (DOD) components in the performance of operations involving munitions in accordance with reference (b).

        (b) It is the policy of the Secretary of the Navy (SECNAV) that the Department of the Navy (DON) follows the instructions of the SECDEF in these matters to the maximum extent practicable.

        (c) It is the policy of the Commandant of the Marine Corps (CMC) that the Marine Corps follow the instructions of the Chief of Naval Operations (CNO) in these matters to the maximum extent possible, unless otherwise specified in this Order.

        (d) When DOD munitions are located in overseas areas, the provisions of this Order shall apply except when compliance with more restrictive local standards is made mandatory by an appropriate international agreement.

        (e) Operations conducted at installations under the command of another Service shall be in accordance with the policy and regulations of the host Service, with the exception of requesting munitions disposition instructions and malfunction and mishap reporting.

    b. In case of conflicting policies or regulations, the most stringent policy/regulation shall apply. Report conflicting policies, by the most expeditious means possible, to the Commander, Marine Corps Systems Command (COMMARCORSYSCOM) Code 204 PM Ammo.

5. Administration and Logistics

    a. Commandant of the Marine Corps Safety Division (CMC SD)
Responsibilities. Provide overall administration of the Marine
Corps Explosives Safety Program.

    b. Deputy Commandant for Combat Development and Integration
(DC CD&I) Responsibilities

        (1) Provide/publish policy and procedures for Marine
Corps ground range and aviation range safety.

        (2) Serve as the single point of contact for range
operations involving the use of Class V(W) and Class V(A)
materiel within the Marine Corps.

        (3) Provide range certification/recertification and
range Technical Assistance Visits (TAVs).

    c. Deputy Commandant for Aviation (DC AVN) (ASL)
Responsibilities

        (1) Serve as the single point of contact for aviation
operations explosives safety as delegated by CMC SD to include
Class V(A) ordnance safety, and operational use of Class V(A)
ordnance in aircraft operating areas (AOA).

        (2) Provide amplifying instructions to policies
involving the safe use of Class V(A) ordnance in the AOA and the
qualification/certification of aviation ordnance personnel.

        (3) Coordinate with COMMARCORSYSCOM Code 204 PM Ammo in
providing aviation ordnance personnel to assist in executing the
Marine Corps Explosives Safety Program.

        (4) Provide aviation ordnance review of reference (c).

    d. Commander Marine Corps Systems Command (COMMARCORSYSCOM)
Responsibilities

        (1) Implement and execute the Marine Corps Explosives
Safety Program for all explosives safety matters within the
Marine Corps.

(2) Provide management and administration functions for all explosives safety matters involving the use of Class V material within the Marine Corps per reference (d) and this Order.

(3) Provide management and oversight for all Class V(W) operations and for those class V(A) operations covered by reference (d) and this Order.

(4) Provide amplifying instructions necessary to implement policies for the safe management and disposition of Class V(W) materiel, the non-operational use of Class V(A) materiel, and the Marine Corps Qualification and Certification (Qual/Cert) Program.

(5) Provide review and recommendations of approval or disapproval for exemptions to transportation regulations involving the movement of Class V materiel by Marine Corps units, tenants, or other entities physically located on Marine Corps installations.

(6) Provide recommendations and endorsement on Explosives Safety Site Plan requests submitted by Marine Corps installations.

(7) Provide recommendations on and endorsement of requests for exemptions and waivers from explosives safety criteria submitted by Marine Corps installations.

(8) Provide approval/disapproval for non-DOD storage authority on all requests submitted by Marine Corps installations.

(9) Provide approval/disapproval of requests for event waivers submitted by Marine Corps installations.

(10) Establish a Staff Assistance Visit (SAV) Program to assist Marine Corps units involved in the storage of Class V(W) materiel and the non-operational use of Class V(A) materiel.

(11) Provide munitions disposition instructions for all excess, obsolete, unserviceable, and waste Class V(W) munitions.

(12) Provide tactical explosives safety expertise in support of contingencies, combat operations, military operations other than war (MOOTW), and associated training.

e. <u>Deputy Commandant for Installations and Logistics (DC I&L) Responsibilities</u>. Coordinate operational and policy matters relating to Class V(W) materiel with COMMARCORSYSCOM Code 204 PM Ammo to ensure that specific functional area considerations and requirements are addressed.

f. <u>Commander Marine Forces Pacific (COMMARFORPAC) and Commander Marine Forces Command (COMMARFORCOM) Responsibilities</u>

(1) Implement and execute the Marine Corps Explosives Safety Program for all explosives safety matters within respective areas of responsibility.

(2) Provide management and administration functions for all explosives safety matters involving the use of Class V material per reference (d) and this Order.

(3) Provide management and oversight for all Class V(W) operations and for those Class V(A) operations covered by reference (d) and this Order.

(4) Provide amplifying instructions necessary to implement policies for the safe management and disposition of Class V(W) materiel, the non-operational use of Class V(A) materiel, and the Marine Corps Qual/Cert Program.

(5) Provide review and recommendations of approval or disapproval for exemptions to transportation regulations involving the movement of Class V materiel by Marine Corps units, tenants, or other entities physically located on Marine Corps installations.

(6) Provide recommendations and endorsement on Explosives Safety Site Plan requests submitted by Marine Corps installations.

(7) Provide recommendations on and endorsement of requests for exemptions and waivers from explosives safety criteria submitted by Marine Corps installations.

(8) Provide recommendations on and endorsements of non-DOD storage authority on all requests submitted by Marine Corps installations.

(9) Provide recommendations on and endorsements of event waivers submitted by Marine Corps installations.

(10) Establish a SAV Program to assist Marine Corps units involved in the storage of Class V(W) materiel and the non-operational use of Class V (A) materiel.

(11) Coordinate operational and policy matters relating to Class V(W) materiel with COMMARCORSYSCOM Code 204 PM Ammo to ensure that specific functional area considerations and requirements are addressed.

g. Commanding General Marine Corps Installations (MCI) East/West Responsibilities

(1) Implement and execute the Marine Corps Explosives Safety Program, for all explosives safety matters within their respective installations.

(2) Provide management and administration functions for all explosives safety matters involving the use of Class V material per reference (d) and this Order.

(3) Provide management and oversight for all Class V(W) operations and for those Class V(A) operations covered by reference (d) and this Order.

(4) Provide review and recommendations of approval or disapproval for exemptions to transportation regulations involving the movement of Class V materiel by Marine Corps units, tenants, or other entities physically located on Marine Corps installations.

(5) Provide recommendations and endorsement on Explosives Safety Site Plan requests for Marine Corps installations.

(6) Provide recommendations and endorsement on requests for exemptions and waivers from explosives safety criteria on Marine Corps installations.

(7) Provide recommendations and endorsements for non-DOD storage authority on all requests submitted by Marine Corps installations.

(8) Provide recommendations and endorsements for event waivers from Marine Corps installations.

(9) Establish a SAV Program to assist Marine Corps units involved in the storage of Class V(W) materiel and the non-operational use of Class V(A) materiel.

(10) Coordinate operational and policy matters relating to Class V(W) materiel with COMMARCORSYSCOM Code 204 PM Ammo to ensure that specific functional area considerations and requirements are addressed.

h. <u>Installation Commander Responsibilities</u>

(1) Ensure compliance with the instructions contained in this Order.

(2) Publish Standard Operating Procedures (SOPs) that govern explosives operations aboard their installations. For those aviation operations for which technical manuals, and Naval Air Systems Command (NAVAIRSYSCOM) conventional weapons loading manuals and checklists are published, a separate SOP is not required.

(3) Establish an explosives safety program that ensures compliance with reference (d) and this Order.

(4) Designate an individual, in writing, civilian or military, as the Explosives Safety Officer (ESO) for the installation.

(a) The ESO shall be organizationally placed in the installation Safety Office.

(b) Explosives safety shall be the ESO's primary duty.

(c) The ESO shall have direct access to the installation commander on all matters pertaining to explosives safety.

i. Explosives Safety Officer Responsibilities

(1) Serve as the single point of contact for all Class V (A) and Class V(W) materiel safety matters at the installation assigned.

(2) Develop, implement, and manage a robust explosives safety program that complies with the provisions of this Order.

(3) Ensure that Explosives Safety Site Approval Packages are maintained for all locations where Class V(A) and Class V(W) materiel is stored and handled.

(4) Ensure that overall installation operations involving the transportation, storage, handling, and execution of munitions disposition instructions of Class V(A) and Class V(W) materiel are conducted in compliance with applicable directives, and executed in a safe manner.

(5) Provide the installation commander with reasoned, informed advice regarding explosives safety and acceptable levels of risk.

(6) Assure that personnel involved with explosives operations receive required training.

(7) Inspect active explosives operating buildings or workplaces as often as necessary, depending on the hazard associated with the operation, but at least annually.

(8) Conduct pre-operational checks and line checks of explosives operating lines, in conjunction with safety personnel trained to perform safety analyses, as new systems or processes are implemented.

(9) Inspect all explosive storage areas and magazines at least annually to ensure that they comply with explosives safety standards.

(10) Assure all SOPs meet the requirements of reference (e), and are reviewed and approved by the activity Safety Office for incorporation of Occupational Safety and Health Administration (OSHA) requirements.

(11) Monitor the installation's qualification and certification program for compliance with reference (f).

(12) Review all requests for deviation from established explosives safety standards to ensure that they comply with existing safety directives.

(13) Inspect maintenance/repair operations involving hot work, and issue permits as necessary.

(14) Review, in conjunction with the Safety Officer and Fire Department representatives, all facility modification drawings and equipment or tooling drawings used for explosive operations to ensure compliance with safety documents.

(15) Approve, in conjunction with the Safety Officer and Fire Department, the electrical hazard classification for each operating building and maintain the list in the Safety Office.

(16) Monitor ordnance display items to ensure that they are inert and do not contain hazardous materials.

(17) Conduct accident investigations in accordance with reference (c), and report findings to higher authority as required. Maintain records per references (h) and (i).

(18) Maintain the activity's explosives safety publications and applicable explosives safety directives.

(19) Assign safety observers to pier or wharf areas in accordance with reference (d) and this Order.

(20) Monitor the facility grounding/lightning protection program.

(21) Ensure Explosives Safety Self-Assessments (ESSAs) are conducted in accordance with Enclosure (4) to reference (g).

(22) Provide oversight on the explosives safety aspects of munitions responses occurring within their area of responsibility.

j. Ammunition Supply Point (ASP) Officer-in-Charge (OIC) Responsibilities

(1) Inspect all Class V (A) and Class V(W) materiel returned by using units to determine serviceability in accordance with applicable technical manuals.

(2) Formally request an investigation on those items reclassified to an unserviceable condition due to misuse by the organization returning the Class V(A) and Class V(W) materiel.

(3) Request munitions disposition instructions for all excess, unserviceable, obsolete, and waste military munitions.

(4) Ensure the munitions disposition instructions provided by the Designated Disposition Authority (DDA) are carried out as directed.

(5) Ensure all operations involving the storage, handling, transport, security, accountability, and repair of Class V(A) and Class V(W) materiel are conducted in accordance with provisions of this Order and applicable explosives safety directives.

k. Deployed Unit Commanding Officer (CO) Responsibilities

(1) Ensure items are properly prepared for turn-in to storage activities.

(2) Ensure packaging materials, banding, pallets, and appropriate markings and shipping documents are available throughout the deployment.

(3) Ensure that necessary manpower and expertise are devoted for adequate preparation and turn-in.

(4) Ensure explosives operations are conducted in accordance with references (b) and (h).

l. <u>Tenant Unit Commanding Officer Responsibilities</u>. Ensure that OICs of unit commands tasked to requisition, receive, handle, store, or transport Class V (A) and Class V(W) materiel comply with this Order and applicable explosives safety directives.

m. <u>Unit Explosives Safety Representative Responsibilities</u>. Conduct all applicable aspects of the unit's explosives safety program, and serve as liaison between the unit and the installation ESO.

n. <u>Unit Personnel Responsibilities</u>. Personnel assigned to ammunition handling and storage operations are responsible for actions as they relate to the implementation of the policies set forth in this Order.

o. <u>Installation Environmental Office Responsibilities</u>. Provide support to ensure compliance with this Order and the corresponding explosives safety directives.

6. <u>Command and Signal</u>

a. <u>Command</u>. This Order is applicable to the Marine Corps Total Force.

b. <u>Signal</u>. This Order is effective the date signed.

M. M. BROGAN
By direction

DISTRIBUTION: PCN 10210540500

Reports Required

REPORT TITLE	REPORT CONTROL SYMBOL	PARAGRAPH
I. Conditional Exemption Violation	EXEMPT	Chap. 7, par. 13c
II. Uncompleted Work Orders	EXEMPT	Chap. 10, par. 10a(4)(b)
III. Captured Enemy Ammunition Report	EXEMPT	Chap. 12, par. 4b
IV. Technical Intelligence Report	EXEMPT	Chap. 12, par. 4h(1)
V. Scientific and Technical Intelligence Report	EXEMPT	Chap. 12, par. 4h(2)
VI. Preliminary Technical Report	EXEMPT	Chap. 12, par. 4i(3)
VII. Program Administrator's Report (PAR) (RCS DD-M(A)891)	EXEMPT	Chapter 7, par. 19c(2)(f)

Enclosure (1)

RECORD OF CHANGES

Log completed change action as indicated.

Change Number	Date of Change	Date Entered	Signature of Person Incorporated Change

TABLE OF CONTENTS

Chapter 1

General Guidance and Responsibilities

1. Background. The Marine Corps continuously trains and deploys with military munitions. The storage, handling, transportation, and employment of these items are inherently hazardous. Therefore, it is imperative that a safety program designed to minimize the potential hazards be aggressively pursued at all levels.

2. Waivers, Exemptions, and Event Waivers. In the event established explosives safety standards cannot be strictly adhered to, several options are available. Detailed information regarding deviations from explosives safety criteria (e.g., waivers, exemptions, event waivers) is contained in this Order and references (a) and (d). All deviations from explosives safety policies and procedures established therein must be approved in accordance with this Order and reference (d).

    a. Waivers and exemptions will be prepared and submitted in accordance with the provisions of appendix I of reference (d), and figure 1-1 of this Order.

    b. An event waiver is a deviation approved on a case-by-case basis for a particular evolution. This waiver is issued for a limited period to meet a specific, non-recurring readiness or operational requirement that cannot otherwise be satisfied. All event waivers will include a risk management assessment from the responsible ESO. Event waivers for Marine Corps installations will be directed to COMMARCORSYSCOM Code 204 PM Ammo for approval (See figure 1-2) with copies to the Naval Ordnance Safety and Security Activity (NOSSA) and CNO. The preferred method of submission to COMMARCORSYSCOM Code 204 PM Ammo is .PDF attachment to email. A paper copy may be sent by mail as a follow-on document, if requested by COMMARCORSYSCOM Code 204 PM Ammo.

        (1) Event waivers for exercises and operations occurring on Marine Corps installations shall be submitted to COMMARCORSYSCOM Code 204 PM Ammo via the installation commander and the respective Marine Corps Forces (i.e., COMMARFORCOM/PAC) for certification of operational necessity.

(2) Deployed units shall submit event waivers to the Combatant Commander (COCOM) via the chain of command for certification of operational necessity. Information addressees will include DC ASL-30 for aviation ordnance and airfield operations, and DC I&L (LP) for Maritime Prepositioning Force (MPF) operations (See figure 1-2).

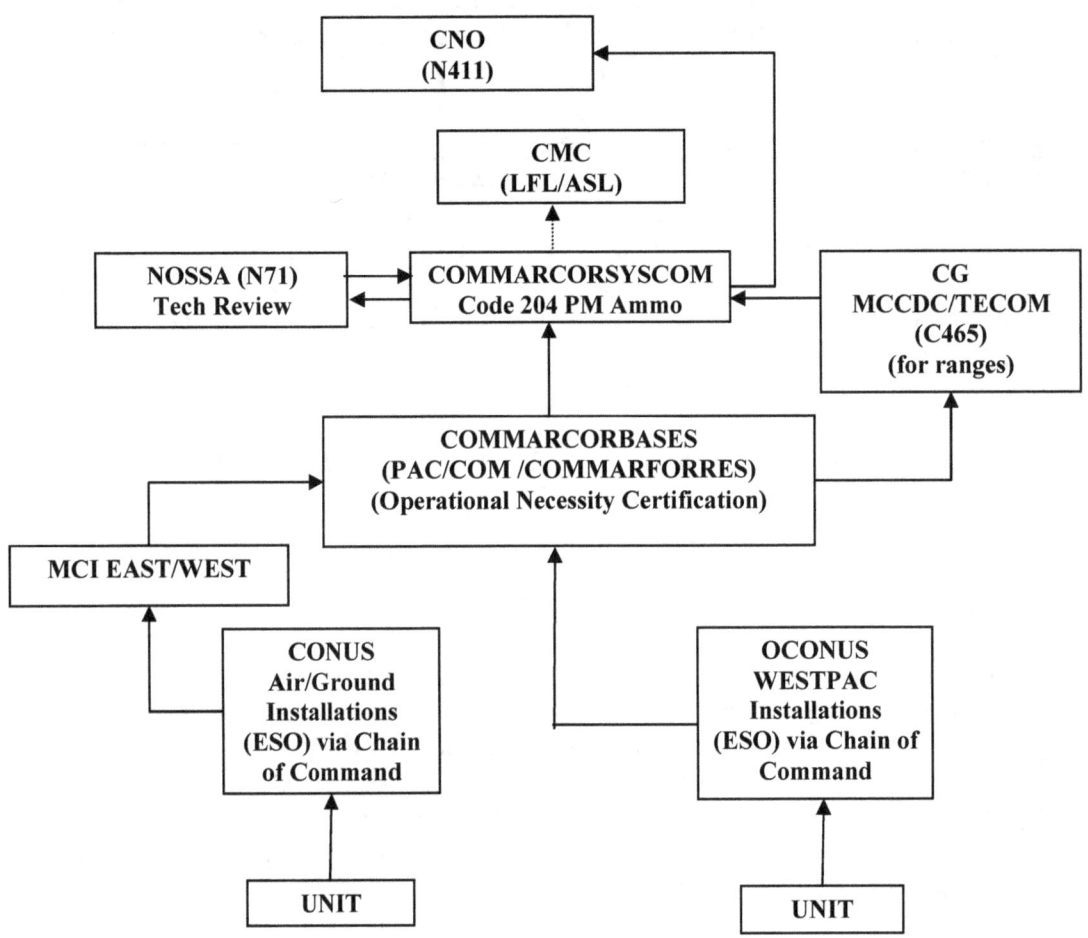

Figure 1-1.--Event Waiver and Exemption Routing for Exercises and Operations on Marine Corps Installations

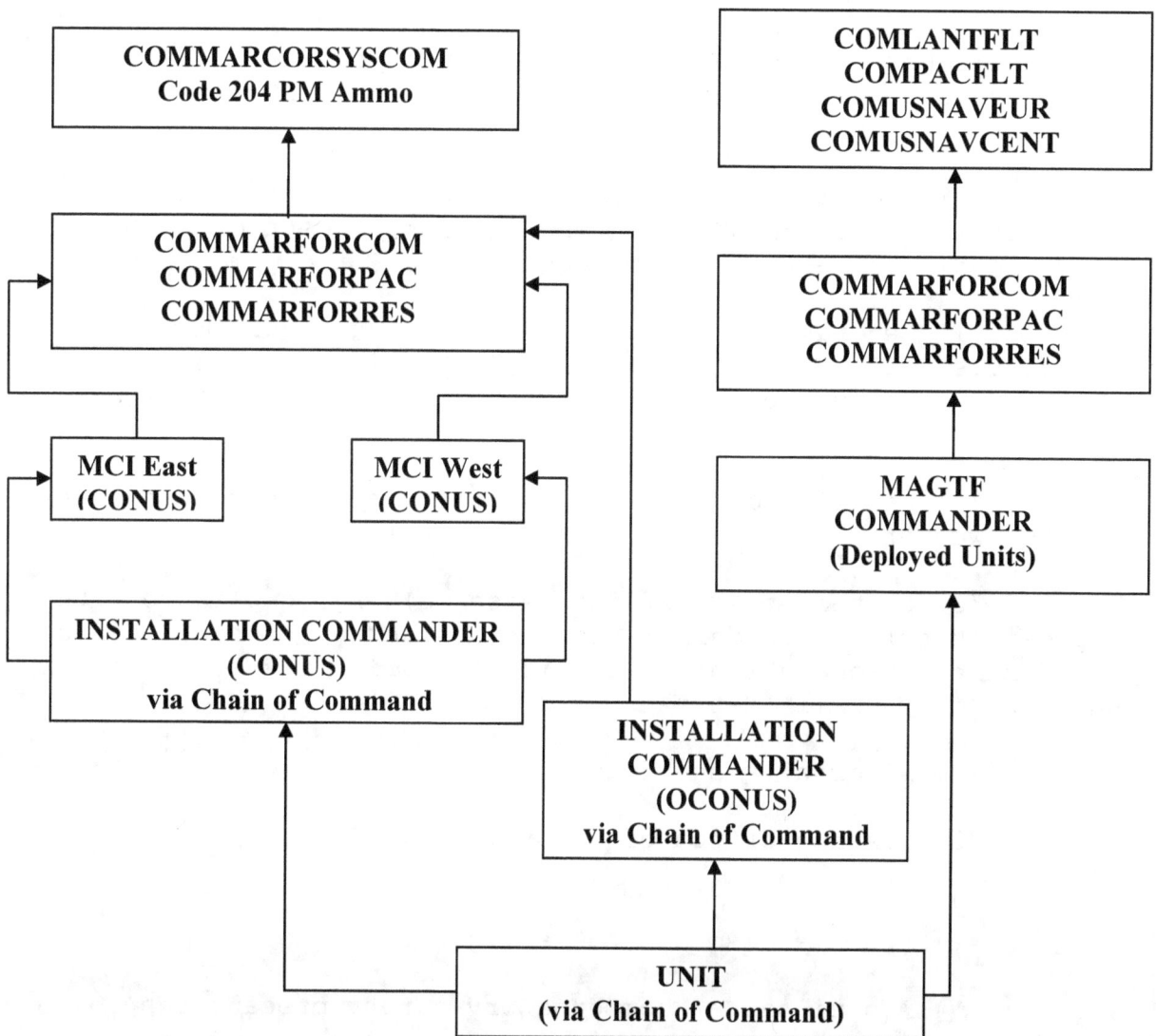

Figure 1-2.--Event Waiver Routing for Deployed Units

Enclosure (1)

(3) Marine activities assigned as tenant commands and activities on other Service bases shall comply with the requirements of the host Service. COMMARCORSYSCOM Code 204 PM Ammo shall be included as an information addressee on all requests for event waivers submitted via a host Service procedure.

c. All requests for event waivers shall contain the following information and will include a statement of operational necessity from the appropriate Force Commander:

(1) General statement of event waiver requirements. Explosives Safety Quantity-Distance (ESQD) information for facilities that may be impacted by the event waiver shall be provided.

(2) Specific description of conditions creating the need for the waiver.

(3) Statement specifying reason(s) why compliance with explosives safety standards cannot be effected. Justification concerning the operational necessity requiring the event waiver shall be provided in detail.

(4) Alternatives examined.

(5) Mission effect of a maximum credible explosives accident.

(6) Risk Assessment Code assigned.

(7) Additional or compensatory safety precautions to be enforced during the waiver period.

3. <u>External Review Boards and Inspections</u>. Representatives from Commandant of the Marine Corps (CMC), COMMARCORSYSCOM Code 204 PM Ammo, Marine Corps Combat Development Command (MCCDC), Department of Defense Explosives Safety Board (DDESB), and NOSSA will make periodic inspections and assistance visits to munitions storage areas at Marine Corps installations to ascertain compliance with prescribed safety regulations. All explosives safety inspections, surveys, and assistance visits to Marine Corps installations by agencies external to CMC and the Commanding General (CG) MCCDC will be coordinated through

COMMARCORSYSCOM Code 204 PM Ammo. Direct liaison from Marine Corps activities to or from DDESB is not authorized, unless initiated by DDESB and coordinated thru COMMARCORSYSCOM Code 204 PM Ammo. Direct liaison between Marine Corps activities and NOSSA, Explosives Safety Support Offices, Atlantic or Pacific Division (ESSOLANT/PAC), or other external organizations on explosives safety matters is also not authorized without coordination and approval from COMMARCORSYSCOM Code 204 PM Ammo. COMMARCORSYSCOM Code 204 PM Ammo will be copied on all explosives safety correspondence from Marine Corps activities to external organizations.

    a. <u>DDESB Surveys</u>. Although DDESB's focus has shifted to the programmatic Service Headquarters level, it will periodically survey selected DOD shore activities involved in handling, processing, or storing munitions. The installation commander is normally notified two to four weeks prior to the scheduled survey. Specific actions to be taken by installation commanders in assisting DDESB, correcting deficiencies, and preparing briefings include the following:

    (1) Provide all information requested by DDESB survey personnel, including station maps, population data, ammunition handling and storage data, and all approved or pending Military Construction (MILCON) site approval data.

    (2) Provide Command representation during the in-brief and debrief.

    (3) Take immediate action to correct obvious and readily correctable violations noted by DDESB.

    (4) Upon receipt of the DDESB survey report, submit a Corrective Action Plan (CAP) via the chain of command to COMMARCORSYSCOM Code 204 PM Ammo within 30 working days. The CAP shall include the following information for all findings:

    (a) Statement of finding.

    (b) Root cause of finding.

    (c) Corrective action taken or planned.

(d) Date corrected or estimated planned correction date.

b. **DDEBS Survey Quarterly Progress Reports for Corrective Action Plans.** Installation ESOs will provide COMMARCORSYSCOM Code 204 PM Ammo with a quarterly progress report on all open uncorrected findings, excluding findings that may require MILCON or major construction to correct, until all findings have been corrected. CAPs will be in the format and contain the information specified in reference (d), and will be submitted via the chain of command.

c. **Explosives Safety Inspection Program.** As directed by CNO, NOSSA will conduct shore station Explosives Safety Inspections (ESIs) at all Navy and Marine Corps installations, including tenant or other commands engaged in the storage, management, accountability, handling, renovation, production, processing, development, testing, or transporting of munitions on a periodic basis.

(1) The procedures required for each installation to be visited by an ESI team are set forth in reference (g). These procedures require specific actions to be taken in providing adequate command attention and support to ESI teams.

(2) ESI team membership will consist of appropriate NOSSA, ESSOLANT/PAC inspector personnel, augmented, as needed, by experts in specific fields selected from various Marine Corps activities, Navy weapons stations, and Navy weapons laboratories. A field grade Marine Corps officer, an Aviation Ordnance Officer (Military Occupational Specialty [MOS] 6502) for aviation installations, and an Ammunition Officer (MOS 2340) for ground installations will be assigned to serve as chief inspector for Marine Corps installations.

(3) With the exception of DOD guidance, Marine Corps orders (MCOs) and directives will take precedence in the event of a conflict with other regulatory guidance.

(a) Differing opinions on regulatory interpretation will be brought to the attention of the Chief Inspector.

(b) The Chief Inspector, drawing from his/her experience and considering inputs from all parties, will make the final decision. If, in extreme instances, the differing views cannot be resolved by the Chief Inspector, the situation will not be written as an ESI finding, but will be written in the report as a separate observation by the Chief Inspector.

(c) The observation will factually describe the regulatory interpretation at issue, present both viewpoints to include applicable regulatory references, and request joint resolution between COMMARCORSYSCOM Code 204 PM Ammo and NOSSA.

(d) Commanders of Marine Corps activities under the cognizance of the ESI Program shall route all correspondence through COMMARCORSYSCOM Code 204 PM Ammo to NOSSA via the chain of command.

d. Inspection of Marine Corps Installations

(1) The inspection of Marine Corps activities conducted in accordance with Program 09 of reference (g) is restricted to military small arms and grenade ranges. Additionally, only the following areas within those eligible ranges may be inspected: off-range ammunition supply points, equipment, operations (including motor vehicles), and ready service lockers and magazines that serve to support range operations.

(2) Inspection of on-range ammunition handling, transportation, range facilities design and construction, and SOPs in support of range operations or field exercises is the responsibility of CG, MCCDC (C465) and is not subject to the ESI Program.

(3) Inspection of Program 08 of reference (g), Arms and Ammunition Security, is not subject to the ESI Program.

(4) Program 07 of reference (g), is not subject to the ESI. Requirements contained in Program 07 are addressed during Environmental Compliance Evaluations, conducted by DC I&L with support from COMMARCORSYSCOM.

e. ESI Quarterly Progress Reports for Corrective Action Plans. Installation ESOs will provide COMMARCORSYSCOM Code 204 PM Ammo with a quarterly progress report on all open uncorrected findings, excluding findings which may require military construction (MILCON) or major construction to correct, until all findings have been corrected. CAPs will be in the format and contain the information specified in reference (g) and be submitted via the chain of command.

    f. <u>Ammunition Hazard Handling Review Board</u>. The purpose of the Ammunition Hazard (AMHAZ) review is to provide a joint review of all factors pertinent to proper safety in the handling, storage, and transportation of munitions at each major installation and all nearby activities. A secondary purpose is to review explosives safety conditions as reflected in, or impacted by, planned construction projects.

    (1) The AMHAZ Handling Review Board is not an investigative or inspection organization. It is an advisory group, dedicated to working jointly with local commands and others to achieve proper balance between operational readiness and acceptable levels of safety.

    (2) The AMHAZ Handling Review Board has authority to recommend to COMMARCORSYSCOM Code 204 PM Ammo, or CNO, the cancellation, modification, or continuation of any waivers or exemptions in effect.

    (3) The procedures required of each installation visited by the AMHAZ Handling Review Board are set forth in appendix J of reference (d). These procedures require specific actions be taken to provide adequate command attention and support to the AMHAZ Review. Commanders of Marine Corps activities under the cognizance of the AMHAZ Handling Review Board shall direct all correspondence to NOSSA via COMMARCORSYSCOM Code 204 PM Ammo via the chain of command.

    g. <u>Environmental Compliance Evaluation</u>. The Marine Corps Environmental Compliance Evaluation (ECE) Program is designed to evaluate every Marine Corps installation on a three-year cycle.

    (1) Those areas impacted by the Munitions Rule (MR) or similar state regulations will be evaluated by COMMARCORSYSCOM Code 204 PM Ammo, while augmenting the DC I&L (LFL) team.

    (2) Protocol for conducting ECEs will be accomplished in accordance with reference (k) and applicable explosives safety regulations.

4. <u>Technical Assistance Visit (TAV)</u>. TAVs are designed to assist in validation of munitions programs associated with the installation and do not serve as a pre-inspection review. There are two types of TAVs. TAVs that address previously identified ESI programmatic issues should be requested from the appropriate NOSSA ESSO as indicated in reference (d). However, any such request will be routed via COMMARCORSYSCOM Code 204 PM Ammo via the chain of command. TAVs relative to day-to-day explosives safety program execution and management (e.g., site plan assistance, files/records) may be requested from COMMARCORSYSCOM Code 204 PM Ammo.

    a. Following are approved procedures to request COMMARCORSYSCOM Code 204 PM Ammo TAVs:

        (1) Requests for TAVs will be submitted electronically (email with attached .PDF signed letter) to COMMARCORSYSCOM Code 204 PM Ammo, Environmental and Explosives Safety (EES) Team at least 60 days prior to the date of the intended visit.

        (2) Requests will include a preferred TAV date and a fall back date.

        (3) Requests will indicate the specific issue to be addressed.

    b. TAVs will not be scheduled within 120 days of a scheduled ESI or other external inspection.

    c. The installation ESO will make available all records, files, documentation, or other materials that may be requested in support of TAVs.

Chapter 2

Transportation

1. <u>Background</u>. Accidents occurring during the movement of munitions can kill and injure personnel, destroy essential supplies, and damage valuable equipment. Therefore, it is imperative that a safety program designed to minimize the potential hazards associated with the transport of munitions be aggressively pursued at all levels.

2. <u>Transportation Modes</u>. Transportation includes movement by any mode (surface or air), whether transported by commercial carrier, Defense Transportation System (DTS), or organic equipment.

3. <u>Transportation Regulations</u>. Regulations pertaining to the motor vehicle transportation of munitions, including authorized vehicles, licensing requirements, and the waiver of these requirements, are contained in reference (d), references (l), (m), and (o) through (w).

4. <u>Rail Transportation</u>. Transportation of munitions by rail shall be in accordance with references (d), (l), (m), (o), and references (r) through (u).

5. <u>Air Transportation</u>. Air shipments of munitions shall be in accordance with references (m), (o), (t), (u), (x), and the International Air Transportation Authority (IATA).

6. <u>Water Transportation</u>. Shipments of munitions by water, including Landing Force Operational Reserve Material (LFORM), Mission Load Allowance (MLA), and MPF ships, shall be in accordance with references (d), (l), (m), (n), (r), (v), (y), and the International Maritime Dangerous Goods (IMDG).

7. <u>On-Station Transportation</u>. The on-station transportation of munitions is conducted in accordance with reference (s).

8. <u>Transportation Over Public Highways</u>. Transportation of munitions over public highways is conducted in accordance with references (d), (l), (m), (o), (r), and (w). Commercial carriers will be used for the transportation of munitions to the maximum extent practicable.

9. <u>Safe Haven</u>. COs and OICs of Marine Corps continental United States (CONUS) activities are authorized to grant safe haven or refuge to military and military-sponsored shipments of explosives, hazardous materials, or other sensitive items endangered by civil disturbance, natural disaster, or terrorist activity. Installations that do not have existing sited explosives vehicle holding/parking areas will, to the extent possible, comply with compatibility, ESQD, lightning protection, and security requirements when providing safe haven to explosives loaded vehicles.

10. <u>Use of Government Owned And Operated Vehicles</u>. Government owned and operated vehicles may be used to routinely transport munitions up to 100 miles one way from a Marine Corps installation. However, any such movement requires prior written authorization from the respective installation commander and prior authorization and coordination with local law enforcement agencies.

    a. Infrequent movements of munitions from an installation to destinations in excess of 100 miles one way may be approved by the installation commander.

    b. Repeated use of Government owned and operated motor vehicles for scheduled movements of munitions exceeding 100 miles one way requires the approval of COMMARCORSYSCOM Code 204 PM Ammo.

11. <u>Transportation by Tactical Vehicle</u>. Requirements contained in reference (p) relative to transport by military tactical vehicles may be waived by the installation commander provided that the movement will be over Marine Corps property or public roads of foreign governments where such waivers are not otherwise prohibited by local laws or regulations. Waivers may be granted as follows:

    a. The use of combinations of military tactical vehicles and cargo trailers may be authorized to carry munitions. When transported in this manner, vehicles shall be routed from storage areas directly to training areas. This authorization applies, provided not more than one truck and one trailer comprise a combination.

b. The use of high mobility multipurpose wheeled vehicles, assault amphibious vehicles, 7-ton series vehicles, logistics vehicle systems, and other approved tactical series vehicles may be authorized to carry munitions during training. Compliance with all current regulations pertaining to fire extinguisher requirements and inspection of vehicles prior to and during such use is mandatory. Ammunition unitized on Navy-approved ferrous metal pallets is exempted from the metal-to-metal contact requirement when loaded aboard military tactical vehicles equipped with ferrous metal cargo beds, provided that those unitized loads are properly secured to the bed of the vehicle. This exception applies only to ammunition that is free of exudate and not liable to leakage, dust, powder, or vapor, which risks accidental ignition of explosives materials and/or explosion. Unpalletized ammunition packed in ferrous metal containers can also be loaded aboard military tactical vehicles without lining the ferrous metal cargo beds with wooden or non-ferrous metal materials provided that loads are in conformance with an existing DOD load drawing, and the ammunition is free of exudates, and not liable to leakage, dust, powder, or vaporize.

c. Plastic bed liners can generate static electricity and are not authorized for use in the transport of scrap explosives. All other types of munitions may be transported in vehicles with plastic bed liners provided they are in their authorized shipping configuration, and secured in the bed to prevent movement.

d. Military tactical vehicles are authorized for off-station transport of munitions. When transportation by tactical vehicle is necessary, loads will be loaded, blocked, and braced, and tied down in accordance with U.S. Army Military Standard (MIL-STD) drawings. Army drawings may be obtained through the Defense Ammunition Center (DAC) website.

e. Use of Marine Corps-owned Compressed Natural Gas (CNG) fueled pick-up trucks for the transport of munitions, both on and off station, is authorized in accordance with safety instructions provided in reference (t). Vehicle design must be approved by the Transportation Equipment Management Center, Naval Facilities Engineer Command (NFEC). Liquefied petroleum gas, propane, or butane may be used as a vehicle fuel source when it is in fuel tanks that are external to the cargo space, and it complies with the vehicle safety requirements of references (d) and (w).

12. Combat Loading

    a. Installation commanders are authorized to approve transportation of live ammunition and crews in the same combat vehicle, subject to the following:

        (1) Authorization is limited to live fire-training areas only. Transportation of ammunition and personnel in the same vehicle en route to training areas is prohibited, as is the transportation of personnel who are not directly assigned responsibilities that require their presence.

        (2) When applicable, ammunition must be transported in original containers. Special attention must be given to securing separately loaded projectiles and propelling charges.

        (3) No smoking restrictions must be strictly enforced.

        (4) All other pertinent safety precautions (e.g., availability of fire extinguishers) must be emphasized to all concerned prior to each evolution.

    b. Operators of vehicles that are an integral part of a tactical weapon system receive explosives training and qualification through completion of MOS-producing schools, and thus may be exempted from the explosives driver's certification process. This is known as combat loading and only applies when the vehicle is tactically configured on a designated range. This does not extend to such vehicles used to transport munitions off-range such as when drawing munitions from or making turn-ins to the ASP. These operations require full compliance with the remaining requirements of this chapter. The decision to exercise the combat loading exemption is at the discretion of the installation commander of the training site.

13. Helicopter Training Operations. Limited quantities of small arms, pyrotechnics, and smoke grenades may be transported with Marines during helicopter training operations. These items shall be limited to ammunition physically carried by Marines as part of the training operation. In addition, all items carried by Marines must be Hazards of Electromagnetic Radiation to

Ordnance (HERO) safe, per reference (x). Palletized ammunition shall not be transported internally or externally with passengers aboard the helicopter during training operations.

14. <u>Explosives Driver/Material Handling Equipment Operator Licensing Requirements</u>. All drivers and operators of explosives material handling equipment (MHE) will be licensed as follows:

a. <u>Explosives Loaded Vehicles</u>. Military vehicles transporting munitions on and off military installations shall be driven by operators who have satisfactorily demonstrated the standards and procedures for transportation of munitions with the following exceptions:

(1) When personnel over the age of 21 are not available, mature individuals ages 18 to 20 may be authorized for on-installation explosives driver qualification. Installation commanders may waive the minimum age licensing requirements within their installations or over public roads of foreign governments, provided that no local civilian or military laws or regulations prohibit such a waiver.

(2) Installation commanders may authorize use of organic equipment for transportation of small arms and associated ammunition for marksmanship training, competition, or other requirements on a case-by-case basis without the usual transportation restrictions. Ammunition must be in the custody of a designated individual. Use of privately owned vehicles may be authorized for use on or off installation.

(3) Personnel to be licensed for tactical vehicles must meet minimum requirements for physical safety standards addressed in reference (z).

(4) Civilian and military explosives drivers will be licensed for a period of two years in accordance with reference (z), and explosives operators of MHE will be licensed for a period of three years, in accordance with reference (aa). Both motor vehicle drivers and MHE operators must possess a valid license with hazardous material endorsement, current medical certificate, and current required training.

b. <u>DON Explosives Safety Training Requirements</u>. Appendix D of reference (d) defines DON explosives safety training requirements. Marine Corps personnel within MOSs 2305, 2311, 2336, 2340, 6017, 6087, 6502, 6531, 6541, and 6591 have satisfied the requirement of the Basic Explosives Safety Course (AMMO-18) through completion of their respective MOS schools. Additionally, personnel holding a 3531 MOS and possessing a valid HAZMAT endorsement are considered to have met the requirements of appendix D. Accordingly, the requirement for Marine Corps explosives MHE operators and explosives drivers to attend AMMO-18 is recommended, vice mandatory. This supersedes the mandatory requirement in Table D-1 of reference (d). AMMO-18 is required for all other personnel, outside the MOSs listed above, who hold a military driver's license with an explosives endorsement.

Chapter 3

Storage and Handling

1. Background. The Marine Corps stores less than 6 percent of its munitions inventory at Marine Corps facilities with the majority being stored at larger Army and Navy ammunition facilities. Munitions are also stored aboard amphibious ships, and aboard Maritime Prepositioning Ships (MPS). For Marine Corps activities, the storage of munitions ashore is generally divided into three broad categories: permanent storage, field storage, and other storage. Regardless of category, proper authority at designated levels must be obtained prior to commencing munitions operations or storing Class V.

2. Storage Facilities. Marine Corps munitions will be stored in permanent magazine storage facilities. Outdoor storage is not authorized except in conjunction with training and field exercises or temporary (overnight) operational circumstances. Permanent magazine storage facilities are those built to Naval Facilities Engineering Command (NAVFACENGCOM) specifications, approved by DDESB, identified in the Installation Master Plan, and maintained and supported by host maintenance departments. Detailed discussions of the various types of existing magazines that may be found at storage facilities are contained in chapter 8 of reference (d). Storage in these facilities shall be in accordance with reference (d) and this Order.

3. Storage of Non-DOD Munitions. Non-DOD (including captured enemy ammunition) and foreign munitions shall be properly segregated and separated from DOD munitions as described in reference (d) and chapter 12 of this Order. The following additional regulations shall be adhered to:

    a. During peacetime, only Class V authorized by formally established requirements or other cataloged items held for another DOD military Service may be stored on Marine Corps installations or in a Marine Corps ASP.

    b. Storage of non-DOD and foreign munitions, with the exceptions of safe haven and combat operations, requires storage authority from COMMARCORSYSCOM Code 204 PM Ammo. Requests may be submitted in either naval message, letter, or electronic mail formats, routed through the local chain of command, to

COMMARCORSYSCOM Code 204 PM Ammo. COMMARCORSYSCOM Code 204 PM Ammo will review and provide approval back to the installation. All requests must include the following:

        (1) Complete item description and National Stock Number (NSN) or other identifying information, if known.

        (2) Item quantity.

        (3) Hazard classification/division (HC/D) and Storage Compatibility Group (SCG), or interim hazard classification documentation.

        (4) Net Explosive Weight (NEW).

        (5) Justification for and type of storage required.

        (6) Expected duration of storage.

        (7) Pre-approved post exercise munitions retrograde plan for unexpended ammunition.

    c. Actual usage of non-DOD munitions aboard Marine Corps installations will require approval from COMMARCORSYSCOM (Code 00T).

    d. Confiscated small arms ammunition items may be stored on Marine Corps installations with approval of the installation commander. Installation commanders may assist external organizations (e.g., Naval Criminal Investigative Service [NCIS], Federal Bureau of Investigation [FBI], local law enforcement) in storage of confiscated or evidentiary small arms ammunition. However, the organization requesting assistance is responsible for providing an accurate inventory of the material and is responsible for proper disposition of the material. These items are not authorized for subsequent issue or use. The organization requesting assistance is responsible for providing proper disposition of the ammunition within 30 days of its release by the investigative authority, or formally requesting that the installation extend storage assistance for a limited, specified period of time while disposition is arranged. Should the organization fail to take either of these actions, the installation will contact the DDA for guidance. The records created in paragraphs 3b, c, and d must be retained and not destroyed.

e. The temporary storage or disposal of non-DOD and/or foreign explosives is available in order to protect the public or to assist agencies responsible for Federal, State, or local law enforcement in storing or disposing of non-DOD and/or foreign explosives when no alternate solution exists. Such storage or disposal shall be established in accordance with an agreement between the SECDEF and the head of the Federal, State, or local agency concerned. These requests will be forwarded to COMMARCORSYSCOM Code 204 PM Ammo who will, in turn, coordinate with DC CL and DC I&L, and with NOSSA, OPNAV, and SECNAV for approval.

4. <u>Marine Corps Tenant Units on Navy Installations</u>. For Marine Corps units located as tenant units aboard Navy installations, munitions storage authority must be requested through the installation commander and forwarded through the Navy chain of command.

5. <u>Supervision of Handling Personnel</u>. Close supervision of personnel involved in munitions evolutions must be maintained at all times in accordance with reference (f).

6. <u>Instruction of Handling Personnel</u>. All personnel handling munitions, including those who utilize munitions in accomplishment of their mission (e.g., tank, artillery, mortar crewman, and engineers), shall be properly instructed prior to each handling evolution. This shall include instructions on the employment and safety precautions associated with the specific items being used. Personnel involved in actual firing or employment of ammunition should refer to reference (ac) or appropriate technical and field manuals for associated safety regulations.

7. <u>Protection from Hazards of Electromagnetic Radiation to Ordnance</u>. Munitions must be protected from the adverse effects of HERO; i.e., transmitting equipment capable of generating electromagnetic radiation of sufficient magnitude to initiate electro-explosive devices (EED). Details regarding electromagnetic radiation are contained in Volume 2 of reference (x).

8. Handling Operations in Aviation Areas. All explosive operations and handling evolutions conducted in combat aircraft loading areas, hazardous cargo areas, flight lines, weapons assembly areas, flight line ready service storage areas, and arm/de-arm areas shall be conducted in accordance with references (d) and (ac), published SOPs, applicable aircraft weapons/stores loading manuals, and Naval Air Training and Operational Procedures Standardization (NATOPS) manuals checklists.

Chapter 4

Security and Accountability

1. Background. Careless losses, improper disposition, theft, and unauthorized use of ammunition expose the public to unnecessary hazards. Therefore, it is imperative that the provisions of this chapter and all cited references be closely examined and adhered to.

2. Commandant Marine Corps-Mandated Changes. Reference (q) provides the current guidelines and policies for the security of arms, ammunition, and explosives (AA&E). Recent procedural reviews have resulted in several AA&E security and accountability policy changes, which have been incorporated into reference (y).

   a. Certification Screening

      (1) COs and OICs shall ensure that all personnel who account for, maintain, and distribute AA&E in performance of their primary duties are screened in accordance with this paragraph and reference (q). This includes civilians, Explosive Ordnance Disposal (EOD), aviation ordnance personnel, engineers, military police, AA&E officers, armorers/custodians, and ammunition technicians.

      (2) Screening will be conducted annually and will include a review of the Marine's medical records, service record book or officer qualification record, and Provost Marshal Office (PMO) incident reports.

      (3) Personnel who are required to be qualified and certified in their primary duties involving AA&E shall document screening annually in accordance with reference (f). The Qualification/Certification (Qual/Cert) Program management standards include review of individual service record books, A&E handlers physical and a de-certification or revocation of certification process that attains the screening goals desired.

      (4) Letters of designation referencing this Order and signed by the CO and OIC may serve as screening documentation.

(5) All other screening documentation shall be done utilizing the latest version of Personnel Screening for AA&E (NAVMC Form 11386) found in reference (q).

(6) This certification will be maintained as long as these individuals are handling AA&E as their primary duties or until their transfers to other duty stations.

(7) If individuals are assigned primary duties of handling AA&E at the new duty station, re-certification is required.

   b. Failure to Meet Certification Screening Requirements. Commanders will coordinate with CMC (MMEA/MMOA) when requesting retraining or reassignment of Marines who do not meet certification-screening requirements. Reference (ad) contains retraining and reassignment requirements.

3. Munitions Inerting and Display

   a. Only qualified EOD personnel are authorized to conduct inerting and stripping operations of Class V in accordance with references (d) and (ae). Inspection and marking of inert-filled and empty ordnance items shall be in accordance with references (d), (ab), and (af).

   b. Inert munitions do not contain explosive material. Only inert munitions and components shall be used for classroom training, public functions, and patriotic occasions. Additionally, aviation ordnance items used for public display shall be in accordance with references (d) and (ag). Only inert munitions shall be used for displays unless specifically approved by COMMARCORSYSCOM Code 204 PM Ammo. Requests for approval shall be submitted using the event waiver process outlined in chapter 1 of this Order.

   c. Commanders at all echelons shall take immediate action to ensure compliance with this Order for all munitions not properly inspected and marked by EOD.

4. Munitions Sale or Exchange. Military personnel or Government employees shall not give away, offer to sell, sell, exchange, or barter munitions. This general prohibition does not apply to munitions provided by Morale, Welfare, and

Recreation (MWR) activities or stocked within the Marine Corps Exchange System. In addition, military-owned munitions shall not be authorized for firing from privately or personally owned weapons.

5. Clearing Barrels

    a. Clearing Barrels Location. Clearing barrels will be provided at designated weapons clearing locations, which are generally located outside arms rooms and ranges.

    b. Construction

        (1) 30 to 50 gallon container, filled with pea gravel or sand. (Pea gravel has the greatest projectile stopping ability.)

        (2) If sand is used, it must be dry and free of rocks and other debris. Properties of wet sand can cause ricochets. Place dry sand in a plastic bag and tie the bag closed prior to placing into clearing barrel. The owning unit must inspect clearing barrels annually and document the inspection as part of the Magazine Inspection Program.

        (3) GSA approved Commercial-Off-the-Shelf (COTS) clearing barrels may be used. If COTS barrels are used, the unit using/maintaining the clearing barrel will obtain and maintain product test and specification data from the manufacturer for as long as the barrel is in use/service. This data will be made available to the ESO and outside inspection personnel upon request. COTS barrels will be inspected for serviceability and maintained in accordance with manufacturers' specifications. In no case shall COTS barrels be inspected less than annually.

        (4) Locally constructed clearing barrels will have ¾ inch plywood or thick rubber matting covering the interior surface diameter of the container fitted directly behind the lid to reinforce the lid against muzzle blast (not applicable to COTS).

        (5) Locally constructed barrels will be at least 14 inches wide, 24 inches deep, and be mounted at a height and angle to permit safe and smooth firearms clearing.

(6) Locally constructed barrels will have an aiming point in the center of the lid at least 4 inches in diameter (not applicable to COTS).

(7) Clearing barrels will be painted red in color with yellow 1-inch stenciling "Weapon Clearing Barrel" on two opposing sides and lid.

(8) Commands must post positive control and procedural guidelines for all weapons at clearing barrels and ensure personnel use them during weapons clearing.

Chapter 5

Site Planning

1. <u>Background</u>. Munitions safety standards contained in reference (b), and implemented by reference (d) and this Order apply to all munitions facilities whenever U.S.-titled ammunition is in the custody of DOD civilian or military employees, and to U.S.-titled ammunition in host nation facilities. These standards shall be considered the minimum, with greater protection provided when practical, and shall govern the siting and construction of all such facilities, unless specifically exempted.

2. <u>Locations Requiring Site Approval/Plans</u>. Site approval is required by references (b) and (d), and this Order for all shore activities at which munitions are handled, manufactured, modified, or stored. This includes permanent fixed containers, not located on ranges, used in conjunction with an amnesty program, as well as those areas used for the storage and permitted treatment of waste military munitions (WMM). Commanders shall request explosives safety site approvals for new construction or modification to existing structures that increases the explosives hazard (e.g., type of munitions, NEW), increases numbers of personnel assigned, or increases the structures' sizes. Commanders shall also request explosives safety site approvals for new construction or modification to existing structures that are encumbered by an ESQD arc. This rule applies to all permanent storage facilities, regardless of the date of first construction, and supersedes paragraph 8-1.2.6.a of reference (d). In the event that a record of site approval is not on file or if the re-designation or modification of an existing site is required, commanders shall submit site approval requests to DDESB via COMMARCORSYSCOM Code 204 PM Ammo. Site approval must be obtained prior to handling or storing Class V, and prior to starting new construction. A permanent storage facility is one that is planned and constructed for extended repetitive use from a specific structure/building, or in support of locations engaged in extended repetitive operations/evolutions. The use of concrete slabs with structures/buildings on it is considered permanent and must be sited regardless of location.

3. Site Approval for Sites Storing less than 300 Pounds Net
Explosives Weight. Site approval for locations storing less
than 300 pounds NEW of Hazard Class/Division (HC/D) 1.2.2, 1.3,
or 1.4 may be obtained from the cognizant ESSOs. Informational
copies of ESSOLANT/PAC approvals will be forwarded to
COMMARCORSYSCOM Code 204 PM Ammo, MCI East/West, and
COMMARFORPAC/COMMARFORCOM.

4. Site Approval for Sites Storing more than 300 Pounds Net
Explosives Weight. Site approval for sites storing more than
300 pounds NEW or for any quantity of HC/D 1.1 or 1.2.1 must be
forwarded to DDESB via the chain of command, via COMMARCORSYSCOM
Code 204 PM Ammo, and via NOSSA.

5. New Construction Encumbered by Existing Arcs. New or
proposed construction, adjacent to explosives storage/operating
areas, that are encumbered by existing approved explosive arcs
require site evaluation by both ESOs and facility planners, and
may require reevaluation/re-siting of those existing explosives
facilities which generated the previously approved arcs.
Careful evaluation by users, facility planners, and ESOs is
essential prior to selecting a site for new construction.

6. Site Approval for Deployed Units. Chapter 11 provides the
field storage and site approval requirements for deployed units.

7. Other Storage

    a. Installation commanders may grant storage authority for
the types and quantities of HC/D 1.3, and 1.4 munitions
identified below in non-sited facilities, such as hangers, troop
buildings, and armories, without regard to ESQD requirements.
However, all storage must comply with fire protection
regulations, safety and physical security requirements outlined
in references (d), (q), and (o), and this Order. Examples
include small arms ammunition, riot control ammunition, and
pyrotechnics for alert, safety or security purposes. Copies of
storage approvals shall be submitted via the chain of submission
depicted in figure 1-2 of this Order.

    b. The following storage authority limitations apply to all
Marine Corps commands, with the exception of Marine Corps
Forces, Reserve (MARFORRES). These limitations shall be
strictly adhered to:

(1) No more than 25 pounds NEW of HC/D 1.4 (see subparagraph (6) below) shall be stored.

(2) No more than 10 pounds NEW of HC/D 1.3 shall be stored.

(3) No HC/D 1.2 materiel shall be stored.

(4) No HC/D 1.1 materiel shall be stored.

(5) When combining HC/D 1.3, and 1.4, no more than 35 pounds total NEW shall be stored, of which no more than 10 pounds NEW shall be HC/D 1.3.

(6) Items hazard-classified as HC/D 1.4S may be stored without regard to limits posted above, and may be excluded from the total NEW.

(7) Installation commanders may grant EOD units authorization to store up to 50 pounds NEW of HC/D 1.3 and 1.4 in EOD operating buildings. This authorization is only to be granted in situations where the items are part of the unit's immediate response tool kit and the total NEW does not exceed 50 pounds per site. However, all storage must comply with fire protection regulations and safety/physical security requirements outlined in references (d), (o), and (q). For existing facilities without sprinkler systems, the total NEW is limited to 25 pounds for overnight storage. The storage of munitions to support EOD training is prohibited per reference (y).

(8) Installation commanders shall review storage authority requests annually. Approval shall be granted only for those types and quantities of munitions required to meet security force, safety, or operational requirements (i.e., burial detail, cartridge actuated device (CAD), or propellant actuated device (PAD) arriving via UPS after working hours). Commanders may also approve storage of privately owned small arms ammunition in unit armories. Privately owned ammunition will be kept segregated from DOD stocks and will be subject to locally written accountability/custody procedures.

(9) Installation commanders shall consolidate all approved storage authorizations and provide this consolidated

listing to COMMARCORSYSCOM Code 204 PM Ammo by 30 June, annually via the chain of command.

8. <u>Special Storage Authority for Marine Corps Reserve Units</u>. Due to unique training and facility restrictions faced by Marine Corps Reserve units, COMMARFORRES may authorize storage of munitions to satisfy local individual unit training requirements, in addition to security-related munitions, with the following restrictions:

    a. Such authority does not conflict with any host installation requirements. In case of a conflict, the most stringent requirements will be observed.

    b. Such authority is granted in support of local training events that necessitate the temporary short-term storage of training assets until such time as they can be transported to an approved storage facility. Such authority shall be reviewed and reissued annually.

    c. Storage of small arms cartridges is authorized in local police facilities only when organic service storage facilities do not afford adequate support.

    d. No HC/D 1.1 or 1.2 munitions is stored.

    e. Storage is limited to HD/C 1.4S, including security and blank funeral ammunition.

    f. Blank funeral ammunition is limited to 80 rounds per detail, based on the estimated number of details conducted annually.

    g. Non-recurring evolutions that require storage of munitions in excess of the requirements outlined above require an event waiver approval by the host installation commander, when applicable, or COMMARCORSYSCOM Code 204 PM Ammo.

    h. An information copy of all storage authorizations shall be provided to COMMARCORSYSCOM Code 204 PM Ammo by 30 June annually.

9. <u>Site Approval Documentation</u>. All documentation for site approval will be routed via COMMARCORSYSCOM Code 204 PM Ammo.

10. <u>Safety Assessment for Explosives Risk</u>. In situations where the siting requirements of Inhabited Building Distance (IBD) cannot be met and all available options have been exhausted, DDESB, in cooperation with all the Services, has approved the use of the quantitative risk management computer model, Safety Assessment For Explosives Risk (SAFER). SAFER provides both acceptable risk criteria, and the statistical methodology necessary to calculate the probability of fatality through data input. Site plans that meet the criteria of SAFER will be approved by DDESB without waiver.

    a. <u>Initial SAFER Submittal</u>. The initial request for a SAFER siting will be developed by a user who has completed training in the latest version of SAFER. The following items must be specifically addressed and included in the SAFER package:

    (1) All elements of a standard site plan submission, to include maps showing the required IBD arcs and all optional locations considered.

    (2) A detailed written explanation of the situation which created the need to deviate from standard Quantity-Distance (QD) criteria, options considered, reasons for rejection of options, and all locations that are effected by the deviation (e.g., building number, usage, sited NEW).

    (3) Copies of the SAFER printouts. The EES team will provide extensive technical assistance with the development of the SAFER submittal. If necessary, a member of the EES team will conduct a TAV to the installation to assist/conduct preparation of the SAFER submittal.

    (4) SAFER site plans will be submitted via the normal site plan submittal chain. Endorsements from the submittal chain will only address command concurrence/non-concurrence with the proposed SAFER site plan. Technical review will be conducted by COMMARCORSYSCOM Code 204 PM Ammo. Once COMMARCORSYSCOM Code 204 PM Ammo has completed a technical review, copies of the SAFER site plan will be submitted to the DDESB Risk Based Explosives Safety Criteria Team (RBESCT) Site Plan Review Panel. Following RBESCT panel review, the review panel chairman will forward the SAFER site plan to DDESB for approval.

b. Recertification of SAFER Site Plans. SAFER site plans are valid for five years, provided there are no changes to conditions identified in the original submission. Upon changes to the original submission, the plan must be resubmitted for approval following the previously stated format. If at the end of the five year period, a newer version of the SAFER software has been developed, a new package must be submitted for approval. If no changes have occurred at the end of the five year time period, the approval may be extended by submission of a letter to COMMARCORSYSCOM Code 204 PM Ammo.

(1) SAFER Recertification Based on Significant Changes to Original Submission. Immediately upon becoming aware of significant changes to the original submission, the installation will immediately notify COMMARCORSYSCOM Code 204 PM Ammo, and prepare and submit a new SAFER site plan. This plan will be prepared using the latest version of SAFER.

(2) SAFER Recertification Based on New Version of SAFER. If a newer version of SAFER has been developed, at the five year period, a package must be prepared using the new software.

(3) SAFER Recertification Based on End of Five Year Time Period. If at the end of the five year time period, there have been no changes to the original submission or updated versions of the SAFER software, then the installation will submit a letter signed by the CO, to COMMARCORSYSCOM Code 204 PM Ammo, confirming no changes have taken place.

11. Forward Arming and Refueling Point Operations. All Forward Arming And Refueling Points (FARPs), in which explosives operations are conducted, must have site approval from the appropriate level of command, as outlined below prior to conducting operations.

a. Training evolutions involving FARP operations, conducted on U.S.-controlled operational training areas/ranges approved for the type munitions being used may be approved by the installation commander. When a FARP operation is established at CONUS locations other than on approved operational training areas/ranges, then formal DDESB site approval is required prior to the conduct of operations. All FARP training operations shall be established in accordance with the separation distances specified in figure 5-1. Units conducting FARP operations shall

conduct all operations, per current NATOPS manuals and
Conventional Weapons Loading (CWL) checklists.

   b. Contingency FARP operations conducted as part of
contingency operations that are not expected to last for more
than 12 months or are of such short-notice that advance approval
is not possible shall be approved by the Unified Commander or
designated Component Commander, as appropriate. Contingency
FARPs shall be established in accordance with the separation
distances specified in figure 5-2. When contingency FARP
operations are expected to last more than 12 months, such
locations require site approval from DDESB. The separation
distances shown are the minimum required to prevent prompt
propagation of explosives sites. However, subsequent reactions
are probable with death to exposed personnel and substantial
damage to assets expected. Aircraft and equipment will not be
usable following such an incident. In order to prevent
propagation or reaction between explosives sites, greater
separation (asset preservation) distances should be provided.
Public Traffic Route (PTR) separation distances will afford this
level of protection.

From:	To:	Rearm Point	Ordnance Staging Area	Ordnance Buildup Area	Ordnance Storage Area	Red Label Area	Sling Out Area	Refueling Point	Bulk Fuel Storage	Bivouac/Billeting Area	Runway/Taxiway (DoD Use)	Runway/Taxiway (Joint Use)	Inhabited Building	Public Traffic Route
Rearm Point		IM	None	IL	IM	IM	IM	IL	IBD	IBD	Note 1	IBD	IBD	Note 3
Ordnance Staging Area		IM	IM	IL	IM	IM	IM	IL	IBD	IBD	PTR	IBD	IBD	Note 3
Ordnance Buildup Area		Note 2	IM	IL	IM	IM	IL	IL	IBD	IBD	PTR	IBD	IBD	Note 3
Ordnance Storage Area		Note 2	IM	IL	IM	IM	IM	IL	IBD	IBD	PTR	IBD	IBD	Note 3
Red Label Area		IM	IM	IL	IM	IM	IM	IL	IBD	IBD	Note 1	IBD	IBD	Note 3
Sling Out Area		IBD	IBD	IBD	IBD	IBD	IBD	IBD	IBD	IBD	Note 1	IBD	IBD	Note 3

Notes:
1. No ESQD applies, however, applicable NAVAIR airfield safety criteria shall be met.
2. K30 used for HC/D 1.1 items only. Use applicable PTR distance for non-mass detonating explosives.
3. PTR distance based on traffic density (low, medium, high). Refer to NAVSEA OP 5, Vol 1, Chapter 7.

Figure 5-1.--Forward Arming and Refueling Point Operation Separation Distances

From:	To:	Rearm Point	Ordnance Staging Area	Ordnance Buildup Area	Ordnance Storage Area	Red Label Area	Sling Out Area	Refueling Point	Bulk Fuel Storage	Bivouac/Billeting Area	Runway/Taxiway (DoD Use)	Runway/Taxiway (Joint Use)	Inhabited Building	Public Traffic Route
Rearm Point		IM	IM	IL	IM	IM	IM	100'	IBD	IBD	K4.5	IBD	IBD	Note 2
Ordnance Staging Area		IM	IM	IL	IM	IM	IM	100'	IBD	IBD	K4.5	IBD	IBD	Note 2
Ordnance Buildup Area		IM	IM	IL	IM	IM	IM	100'	IBD	IBD	K4.5	IBD	IBD	Note 2
Ordnance Storage Area		IM	IM	IL	IM	IM	IM	100'	IBD	IBD	K4.5	IBD	IBD	Note 2
Red Label Area		IM	IM	IL	IM	IM	IM	100'	IBD	IBD	K4.5	IBD	IBD	Note 2
Sling Out Area		IM	IM	IL	IM	IM	IM	100'	IBD	IBD	K4.5	IBD	IBD	Note 2

Notes:
1. Where asset preservation is a primary concern, use K24/K30 separation for H/D 1.1, and PTR separation distance for H/D 1.2, 1.3, or 1.4. Applies wherever IBD is not specified.
2. PTR distance based on traffic density (low, medium, high). Refer to NAVSEA OP 5, Vol 1, Chapter 7.

Figure 5-2.--Forward Arming and Refueling Point Operation Contingency Separation Distances

12. Requirements

   a. Commanding Officer's Requirements for Site Planning

      (1) Ensure a file copy of each site map is maintained, showing the locations of all magazines and magazine areas. In addition, the file will list the type and construction of magazines, the distances to inhabited buildings on and off the installation, public passenger railways, public highways, navigable channels, and Intraline (IL) Distances to explosive operations. The NAVFACENGCOM building numbers shall be indicated for each magazine. The site map shall be revised as often as necessary to maintain accuracy of the data. All site maps should be in 1:400 scale and of sufficient quality to be useable.

      (2) Ensure a file of the appropriate approval documents for all current munitions storage sites is maintained.

      (3) Obtain approval for any new ammunition or explosives storage sites, or modification to existing sites, prior to the start of their construction.

      (4) Obtain approval for construction of any facilities that are unrelated to ammunition and explosives storage and operations, but may be affected by these storage and operations (i.e., within an IBD arc) prior to the start of construction.

   b. Facilities Planning/Public Works Requirements for Site Planning. Facility planners are responsible for preparing and routing all planned construction projects, of both explosives and non-explosives facilities, that may encumber explosive operations, or that violate existing ESQD arcs through the installation Explosives Safety Office for ESO review, recommendations, and concurrence. Planners are responsible for preparing and forwarding all site plans and approval requests, providing all maps, blueprints, and construction details required by ESO, higher headquarters, and DDESB review authorities. The site approval process is complex and requires time. Both engineering and explosives safety requirements are reviewed by several different organizations prior to final review/approval by DDESB. It is not uncommon for this process to take more then 12 months, depending on workload of review organizations. It is, therefore, required that facility planners submit site packages as early in the development stages of a project as possible. No construction will occur prior to the receipt of an approved site plan.

    c. <u>Installation Explosives Safety Officer's Requirements for Site Planning</u>. The ESO is responsible for the following site planning activities:

       (1) Review and provide recommendations for all facility construction, modification, or changes in usage impacting base explosives operations.

       (2) Once correct, sign Block 8 of NAVMC Form 11010/31, Part II, Division A, indicating concurrence of site plan.

       (3) Coordinate with facility planners to develop alternative site plans should original plans be found out of compliance with regulatory requirements.

       (4) Maintain accurate and up-to-date files of all approved site plans.

    d. <u>Ammunition Officer's Requirements for Site Planning</u>. Ammunition Officers are responsible for developing preliminary requirements for construction, modification, or changes in use of facilities to meet mission goals, and submitting these requirements through the appropriate channels for formal development. Ammunition Officers work with ESOs, facility planners, and installation Environmental Offices to ensure that all requirements of these offices are included.

    e. <u>Installation Environmental Office's Requirements for Site Planning</u>. The Environmental Office is responsible for coordinating with the ESO and ammunition personnel to ensure that all proposed construction, modification, or change in usage of explosives facilities comply with applicable Federal, DON, Marine Corps, State, and local environmental regulatory requirements. The Environmental Office will prepare all required regulatory documentation, studies, and reports relative to these requirements. The installation Environmental Office should be consulted early in the process to ensure sufficient time for preparation of any required environmental documents.

13. <u>Instances Requiring Site Approval</u>

a. Site and general construction plans shall be submitted for review and approval for new construction of:

(1) Ammunition explosives facilities.

(2) Non-ammunition explosives facilities within QD arcs.

(3) Facility modifications, change of mission, or change of operations that increase explosives safety criteria.

(4) Vulnerable facility construction. Although site plans for construction of vulnerable facilities located on a DOD installation that are outside but near QD arcs are not required, it is recommended that they be submitted to DDESB for review and comment.

b. These examples are not designed to be all inclusive. Any questions should be referred to COMMARCORSYSCOM Code 204 PM Ammo.

14. <u>Instances Not Requiring Site Approval</u>

a. Site and general construction plans need not be submitted for facility modifications that do not increase the footprint of the facility, result in an increase in explosives hazards or NEW, or increase the numbers of personnel assigned to the facility.

(1) Certain activities do not require a site plan. They include routine maintenance, repair work, and up-keep that is performed on a regular basis where workers will be within K18 distance from a Potential Explosion Site (PES) for short periods of time.

(2) The following actions, while not requiring a site approval, will require an Explosives Event Waiver, if encumbered by K18 ESQD arcs:

(a) Utility line servicing, or floor or roof repairs.

(b) Casualty or emergency situations requiring minor repairs to restore the facility to its original condition.

(c) Non-routine maintenance and repair projects of longer duration, provided there is no increase in the number of personnel exposed to an explosives hazard after project completion, the footprint of the facility is not increased, there is no increase in the sited explosives weight of the facility, and there is no change in the HC/D of the material stored.

b. These examples are not designed to be all inclusive. Any questions should be referred to COMMARCORSYSCOM Code 204 PM Ammo.

Chapter 6

Amnesty Program

1. <u>Background</u>. The physical security and accountability of munitions are of paramount importance. While strict adherence to the provisions of chapter 4 will safeguard against the intentional acts, measures are necessary to supplement the process, thereby ensuring maximum recovery of munitions items outside the supply system. A munitions amnesty program can help satisfy this requirement. This chapter sets forth the guidelines and procedures for the Marine Corps Amnesty Program.

2. <u>Amnesty Program Guidelines</u>. The amnesty program is neither intended to circumvent normal turn-in and accountability procedures, nor serve as a substitute for sound leadership. Implementation of an amnesty program is not mandatory, but subject to the discretion of the installation commander. If implemented, the program is established to provide an opportunity for individuals to return munitions that have been stolen, misplaced, or inadvertently left in the possession of an individual. For this program to be effective, returns must be able to be made without fear of prosecution. Therefore, individuals making amnesty turn-ins will not be the subject of investigations. If implemented, each amnesty program is subject to the following guidelines:

    a. All munitions found on installation, excluding small arms ammunition (up to and including .50 caliber), will be considered extremely hazardous and will not be handled or moved by unauthorized personnel. Supporting EOD personnel shall be contacted immediately and will respond upon request to recover this category of munitions. Small arms ammunition may be delivered directly to the ammunition supply point (ASP) or Provost Marshal Office (PMO). Regardless of the turn-in method, neither documentation nor verification of identity is required. Using units discovering munitions after having completed their turn-ins and having their accounts reconciled are not authorized to use the amnesty procedures outlined herein. These units shall make amended turn-ins using the procedures set forth in reference (y).

    b. Civilian law enforcement agencies shall be contacted when any DOD-owned munitions are discovered outside of the installation boundaries. If required, the civilian law enforcement agencies may request EOD assistance through the PMO.

c. To ensure proper control and safety, an amnesty program can be supplemented by any of the following methods, or combinations thereof:

(1) Amnesty days may be scheduled as often as deemed necessary for the collection of unauthorized munitions. Collection points shall only be established at locations that afford IBD levels of protection. To ensure that proper care is exercised, qualified and certified ammunition or EOD personnel must be available and on-hand to supervise amnesty turn-ins. The installation ESO will approve the location of all potential collection points.

(2) Installation commanders may establish dates and sites which explosives transport vehicles may be dispatched to receive amnesty turn-ins. The location of the amnesty vehicle must be selected so as not to create a hazard to personnel or facilities. At a minimum, locations shall afford inhabited building distance (IBD) protection (e.g., minimum of 1,250 feet from inhabited areas or those frequented by personnel unrelated to explosives operations). Amnesty program vehicles transporting explosives shall use established base explosive transportation routes.

3. Permanently Sited Amnesty Program Containers. Due to the hazardous nature of munitions, the use of amnesty containers is the least desirable method of supporting an amnesty program. If implemented, extreme care must be exercised as to the physical location, numbers, and construction of amnesty containers.

a. Location of Amnesty Program Containers. Permanent off-range locations for HC/D 1.1, 1.2, and 1.3 materials shall be sited in accordance with reference (d), as above-ground unbarricaded magazines and provide IBD protection. Containers for HC/D 1.4S small arms ammunition do not require siting but will be provided a 50 foot fire safety separation. Containers placed on operational ranges approved for the type of ammunition involved do not require a separate site approval as long as its location does not extend an IBD arc beyond established range borders.

b. Construction of Amnesty Program Containers. If used, amnesty program containers are to be constructed of at least 10-gauge steel, permanently mounted, and secured with a lock in accordance with reference (q).

(1) Slots in containers for HC/D 1.4S material will be sized to accept no larger than a .50 caliber cartridge. Containers shall be clearly marked "AMNESTY BOX FOR SMALL ARMS AMMUNITION ONLY-NO SMOKING WITHIN 50 FT."

(2) It is recognized that numerous items of hazard classes/divisions other than HC/D 1.4 may be fitted/forced through a slot designed for .50 caliber ammunition. For this reason it is imperative that daily check personnel adhere to the provisions of paragraph 3.c below.

c. Daily Checks of Amnesty Program Containers. Personnel performing daily checks on amnesty program containers authorized for HC/D 1.1, 1.2, or 1.3 must be qualified and certified in accordance with reference (f). Personnel not qualified and certified in accordance with reference (f) may perform checks of small arms ammunition (HC/D 1.4) amnesty program containers on a daily basis but shall not remove items from the container if munitions items other than small arms ammunition are present. Non-qualified/certified checkers will contact EOD or qualified ASP personnel to remove unauthorized munitions contents in accordance with base procedures. All munitions recovered shall be returned to the installation ASP. Items that appear to be damaged or unsafe to move shall be left in place until examined by EOD.

4. Responsibilities

a. Installation Commander Responsibilities for an Amnesty Program. If an amnesty program is implemented, commanders shall be responsible for ensuring the following:

(1) Periodically brief assigned personnel on the existence and guidelines for use of the amnesty program.

(2) Monitor execution of the amnesty program to ensure guidelines are being properly followed.

(3) Establish Standard Operating Procedures (SOPs) addressing details on implementation of the installation's amnesty program.

(4) Approve, in writing, all physical locations of amnesty program containers. Documentation will be resubmitted if physical locations of containers change, and by each subsequent installation commander. One letter, listing all approved locations, is acceptable. A copy of this letter will be furnished to the ESO, Range Control Officer (RCO), EOD OIC, duty officer, and OIC of the ammunition storage area.

(5) Establish key control procedures for amnesty program containers in accordance with requirements for access to secure areas, and installation orders.

b. <u>Ammunition Personnel Responsibilities for an Amnesty Program</u>. Ammunition personnel responsible for storage, inspection, transport, handling, and packaging of ammunition are responsible for the following:

(1) Monitor amnesty program containers daily and remove any turned-in materiel. Respond to requests from monitoring personnel not qualified/certified to handle or transport munitions, and remove any turned-in material that they may discover. Ensure material is safe for transportation and storage. If condition is in doubt, notify EOD.

(2) Mark and package material for storage and transportation as required.

(3) Request disposition instructions from the appropriate Service designated disposition authority (DDA).

c. <u>Responsibilities of All Personnel Utilizing Munitions</u>. All personnel utilizing munitions are responsible for the following:

(1) Follow established accountability and turn-in procedures for all munitions in their possession.

(2) Take special precautions to ensure munitions are not inadvertently removed from training sites, discarded, or

otherwise misdirected to circumvent established munitions turn-in and accountability procedures.

    (3) Understand the installation amnesty program.

    d. <u>Responsibilities of the Explosives Safety Officer</u>. The installation ESO will advise the installation commander on location/siting of amnesty containers and monitor the execution of the amnesty program. Monitoring may be accomplished through the following activities:

    (1) Review of SOPs.

    (2) Periodic review of key control logs/documents to ensure daily checks are being accomplished.

    (3) Physical inspection of amnesty containers annually.

    (4) Review of amnesty program turn-in procedures.

    (5) Documentation of all reviews and inspections via locally developed checklist. Reviews/inspections may be conducted in conjunction with other inspections. If review/inspection is conducted independently from other inspections, document the review/inspection separately and maintain documentation for two years. If review/inspection is conducted in conjunction with another inspection, ensure that the amnesty program inspection points are included on the appropriate inspection checklist.

Chapter 7

Unserviceable and Waste Military Munitions Management

1. Background. The 12 February 1997 Military Munitions Rule
(MR), reference (ah), in part, establishes criteria under which
munitions are regulated as waste. Largely as a result of DOD's
effective munitions management practices, including storage,
transportation, and explosives or munitions emergency response,
the Environmental Protection Agency (EPA) incorporated several
existing DOD munitions management practices into the MR.

2. Goal. It is a Marine Corps goal to:

    a. Maximize the use of valuable and limited Marine Corps
munitions through:

        (1) Intended use.

        (2) Legitimate emergency destruct and combat disposal
(ED/CD) training.

        (3) Maintenance and renovation.

        (4) Recycling and recovery of chemicals and components.

        (5) Sales to Foreign, Federal, State, and/or local
organizations.

    b. Ensure unused munitions are never buried (with the
intent to discard), abandoned, or otherwise disposed of.

    c. Comply with applicable Federal, State, DOD, DON, and
USMC explosives safety and environmental requirements, while
minimizing waste military munitions (WMM) generation.

    d. Transport WMM to Resource Conservation and Recovery Act
(RCRA)-permitted treatment, storage, or disposal facilities.

    e. Coordinate with DC I&L on WMM matters to include
explosives or munitions emergency responses.

3. Munitions Disposition Process

     a. Munitions Disposition Process. The Munitions
Disposition Process is a two-step process consisting of a
disposition request and subsequent instructions. The DDA is
responsible for providing disposition instructions for
unserviceable munitions and WMM. Disposition instructions may
assign an Ammunition Condition Code. Ammunition Condition Code
"H" refers to the condition of ammunition that is restricted
from being used for its primary purpose. However, Ammunition
Condition Code "H" ammunition is not WMM, since it may be
legitimately used in training in support of Individual Training
Standards (ITSs) or transported to an authorized facility for
reuse, recovery, or recycling. Ammunition Condition Code "V" is
used to designated WMM. This code is not normally applicable to
EOD explosive or munitions emergency response. Absent an
explosives or munitions emergency, whenever abandoned or buried
unused munitions have been recovered, personnel will contact the
DDA for guidance and/or disposition instructions.

     b. Ammunition Support Activity Requests for Munitions
Disposition Instructions. The installation or ammunition
support activity possessing unserviceable munitions or WMM will
usually initiate the Munitions Disposition Process by requesting
munitions disposition instructions from the appropriate DDA.

          (1) Requests for disposition instructions for Class V(W)
materiel in Ammunition Condition Code "H" or Ammunition
Condition Code "V" will be sent to the Marine Corps DDA. If e-
mail is unavailable, a standard naval message will be sent to
COMMARCORSYSCOM QUANTICO VA//AM-EES//. Disposition requests for
Class V(W) materiel in all other Ammunition Condition Codes will
be sent to COMMARCORSYSCOM Code 204 PM Ammo, Inventory
Management (IM) Team.

          (2) Class V(A) disposition requests will be sent to the
Navy DDA at NAVSURFWARCENDIV CRANE IN//PM-42// via a standard
naval message.

     c. Coordination

          (1) The DDA will coordinate with Inventory Management
(IM) when appropriate. The DDA will provide munitions
disposition instructions within 60 days of receiving each

disposition request. Item Manager (IM) or DDA munitions disposition instructions will provide direction for the effective and compliant management of Class V(W) materiel as assets become available.

(2) IM will provide specific shipping and funding documents in accordance with the DDA's instructions.

d. Recordkeeping Requirements for Munitions Disposition Instructions. The ammunition support activity will maintain munitions disposition instructions per reference (h), SSIC 8020.1.

4. Munitions Disposition Request. Request for munitions disposition instructions will contain the following information:

a. The Department of Defense Identification Code (DODIC) for each item.

b. Quantity.

c. Ammunition Condition Code.

d. The applicable Notice of Ammunition Reclassification (NAR), Ammunition Information Notice (AIN), or reason for local Ammunition Condition Code change.

e. The potential for local use by ammunition technicians, combat engineers, and/or EOD personnel in ED/CD or destruction of Captured Enemy Ammunition (CEA). If the ammunition support activity's request for munitions disposition instructions also contains a request to conduct ED/CD or CEA training, the request will state the approximate date of the training and the anticipated number of personnel to be trained. Additionally, in a separate paragraph, this request will identify the type and quantity of donor materiel required. If donor materiel is required, ensure the request includes CG Training and Education Command (TECOM), Quantico, VA (C465) as an information addressee. The DDA will provide a coordinated response. If the request is sent via e-mail, the DDA will coordinate the special allowance for donor material with TECOM.

f. Additional information pertinent to the request or situation surrounding the request.

g. A local point of contact.

5. <u>Munitions Disposition Instructions</u>

a. <u>DDA Disposition</u>. The DDA's munitions disposition instructions may include variations of the following directions:

(1) <u>Shipment to Designated Depot or Other Capable Activity</u>. IM will provide document numbers for the shipment of Class V(W) materiel in the munitions disposition instructions.

(2) <u>Authorization to Conduct Emergency Destruction/ Combat Destruction or Captured Enemy Ammunition Training</u>. The authorization to conduct ED/CD or CEA training will list DODICs, quantities, and any other pertinent information.

(3) <u>Management as Waste Military Munitions</u>. In the event Class V(W) materiel is designated as WMM, the DDA will include specific guidance in the munitions disposition instructions.

(4) <u>Appropriate Change of Ammunition Condition Code</u>. The DDA will identify the applicable Ammunition Condition Code for all munitions addressed on the disposition request.

b. <u>Coordinating Instructions</u>. Although many munitions disposition instructions are routine, unique situations may require coordination with organizations internal and external to the Marine Corps. The DDA will provide coordinating instructions as required.

6. <u>Misfires</u>. Misfires considered both safe to transport off-range and to store in designated ammunition storage units (ASUs) will be evaluated for repair, reuse, or additional evaluation (e.g., malfunction or misfire investigations, failure analysis, testing for Research, Development, Test & Evaluation [RDT&E] purposes, and evaluation for possible repair or reuse). These munitions are not WMM, but will be reclassified into the appropriate condition code after evaluation is complete. Following evaluation, the ammunition support activity possessing

the munitions may need to request munitions disposition instructions.

7. <u>Recovered Military Munitions</u>. Recovered unused munitions are divided into two categories: those that were intentionally abandoned, and those that were not.

    a. <u>Abandoned and Subsequently Recovered Unused Waste Munitions</u>. Unused munitions that have been buried or abandoned with intent to discard will be managed as WMM.

        (1) Recovered WMM will be accumulated in authorized WMM storage magazines, and the cognizant ammunition support activity will request munitions disposition instructions from the DDA within 96 hours after the recovery.

        (2) WMM shall not be destroyed without munitions disposition instructions unless EOD declares an explosive or munitions emergency.

    b. <u>Recovered Unused Munitions</u>

        (1) When unused munitions are recovered, EOD should be immediately notified if the condition of the munitions is in doubt. Absent an explosive or munitions emergency response the unused munitions should be placed in a storage magazine.

        (2) The installation ammunition support activity should immediately notify the installation Environmental Office and the DDA for disposition instructions.

8. <u>Emergency Destruct/Combat Disposal and Captured Enemy Ammunition Training</u>

    a. Unserviceable munitions will be considered for ED/CD and CEA training when a training requirement is identified in the request for munitions disposition instructions. The DDA will examine DODICs and quantities to ensure compliance with reference (af) requirements.

    b. Ammunition support activities requesting authorization to conduct ED/CD and CEA training will ensure that ED/CD and CEA training is pre-planned and documented according to local SOPs and personnel participating in ED/CD and CEA training have their

training documented. These records are subject to inspection
and evaluation and must include:

    (1) The names of personnel trained.

    (2) The training date(s).

    (3) The purpose of the training supported by lesson
plans, local SOPs, and training standards being met.

    (4) The types and quantities of munitions used.

9. Foreign Military Munitions Management

    a. Marine Corps units training with foreign militaries on
Marine Corps operational ranges require a pre-approved plan for
retrograding unused and unserviceable foreign military
munitions.

    b. The hosting command will ensure that users of foreign
military munitions on Marine Corps operational ranges have a
pre-approved plan for retrograding unused and unserviceable
foreign military munitions within 30 days after completion of
military training with the foreign military munitions.

    c. Foreign military munitions remaining on a Marine Corps
installation after final execution of the retrograde plan fall
under the installation's cognizance.

    d. Within 30 days after final execution of the retrograde
plan, the cognizant installation shall request munitions
disposition instructions for them. The Marine Corps DDA will
provide disposition for Class V(W) materiel. The Navy DDA will
provide disposition for Class V(A) materiel. See chapter 3 of
this Order for requesting non-DOD munitions storage
authorization.

10. Standard Operating Procedures. Ammunition support
activities will establish and maintain current SOPs as specified
in references (d) and (e), and this Order. Each installation's
Environmental Office and ESO will evaluate the installation's
SOP on WMM procedures to ensure explosives safety and regulatory
compliance. In addition to the requirements found in the
references above, each SOP will contain:

a. Procedures for requesting, executing, and maintaining munitions disposition instructions.

b. Procedures for conducting ED/CD and CEA training.

c. Management plans for WMM based on the type storage or accumulation available (e.g., Conditionally Exempt (CE) WMM storage, RCRA-permitted WMM storage, or less than 90-day WMM accumulation). Activities accumulating and facilities storing WMM must comply with applicable Federal, State, and/or local hazardous waste management requirements; reference (d); and this Order.

d. WMM quarterly inspection and annual inventory procedures. (Note: Regulatory authority may require more frequent inspections.)

e. Contingency plans meeting the requirements of applicable Federal, State, and/or local hazardous waste management requirements, and reference (d).

f. Procedures to ensure hazardous waste management training is conducted in accordance with applicable Federal, State, and/or local hazardous waste management requirements. This training will be documented in individual training records. Most Marine Corps Environmental Offices provide or coordinate hazardous waste management training.

11. Recordkeeping. To comply with explosives safety and environmental requirements pertaining to Class V materiel, the following records, as applicable, will be maintained per reference (h), SSIC 8020.1 following receipt of applicable disposition instructions:

a. Disposition instructions involving Ammunition Condition Codes H and V.

b. WMM quarterly inspections and annual inventories of all WMM. (Note: Regulatory authority may require more frequent inspections.)

c. Explosives safety and environmental compliance evaluations (i.e., audits).

d. Hazardous waste management personnel training records.

e. Hazardous waste manifests.

f. Storage records for WMM stored under CE.

12. <u>Transportation of Waste Military Munitions</u>. WMM will be transported in accordance with applicable Federal, State, and/or local hazardous waste transportation requirements.

a. <u>Conditionally Exempt WMM Transportation</u>. "Conditional Exemption" (CE) is a term used and defined by Federal regulations and the MR for transporting munitions without full adherence to RCRA standards. Subject to more stringent State and/or local hazardous waste transportation requirements, WMM may be transported under a CE without a hazardous waste manifest when all states along the planned shipment route allow CE WMM transportation and the following conditions are met:

(1) The WMM are not chemical agents or chemical munitions.

(2) The WMM are transported in accordance with DOD shipping controls applicable to the transport of munitions from a military owned or operated installation to a military owned or operated hazardous waste treatment, storage, or disposal facility. Shipments to commercial hazardous waste treatment, storage, or disposal facilities are ineligible for CE.

(3) In the unlikely event of loss or theft, the CE transporter immediately notifies the installation Environmental Office and the ammunition support activity so that regulatory authority may be orally notified within 24 hours after the transporter is aware of the loss or theft.

b. Subject to more stringent State and/or local hazardous waste transportation requirements, the transportation CE applies to WMM transported by military personnel or by commercial carriers under contract with the Military Traffic Management Command and operating under the DOD and Department of Transportation (DOT) systems of shipping controls.

c. Subject to more stringent State and/or local hazardous waste transportation requirements, if a receiving military owned or operated hazardous waste treatment, storage, or disposal facility (e.g., a Marine Corps installation; ammunition depot; or government-owned, contractor-operated facility) does not receive the WMM shipped under CE within 45 days after the day of shipment, the Environmental Office of the receiving military owned or operated hazardous waste treatment, storage, or disposal facility will make notifications required by applicable Federal, State, and/or local hazardous waste management requirements.

(1) <u>Loss of Conditional Exemption</u>. If applicable, the failure to comply with any of the conditions listed above would cause the immediate loss of CE. The loss of CE would subject the WMM to full hazardous waste regulation and may result in a regulatory enforcement action.

(2) <u>Conditional Exemption Reinstatement</u>. If the CE is lost for any WMM, the installation Environmental Office will coordinate with the ammunition supply activity and the traffic management office to identify the circumstances of the violation and demonstrate that the violation(s) leading to the loss is/are not likely to recur. After this coordination, the installation Environmental Office may apply to regulatory authority for CE reinstatement.

d. Subject to more stringent State and/or local hazardous waste transportation requirements, WMM transportation within the boundary of an installation is not subject to hazardous waste transporter requirements. Additionally, if the shipment occurs on a public or private right-of-way that is within or along the border of an installation, an RCRA hazardous waste manifest is not required. The installation Environmental Office shall be notified of WMM movement on the installation.

e. Off-site transportation of WMM not shipped under CE must comply with Federal, State, and/or local hazardous waste transporter requirements, and reference (d), and shall be coordinated with the installation Environmental Office.

13. <u>Storage of Waste Military Munitions</u>

MCO P8020.10B
31 OCT 2007

a. <u>Waste Military Munitions Storage Requirements</u>. WMM will be stored in accordance with Federal, State, and/or local hazardous waste storage requirements; this Order; and references (b) and (d). Subject to more stringent State and/or local hazardous waste storage requirements, this section describes minimum CE WMM storage requirements. CE WMM storage is a regulated activity and must be coordinated with the installation Environmental Office. CE WMM storage must also be coordinated with the installation Explosives Safety Office to ensure compliance with explosive safety requirements.

b. <u>Conditionally Exempt Waste Military Munitions Storage</u>. For conventional WMM stored under DDESB jurisdiction, a CE from hazardous waste storage requirements may be granted under the conditions immediately below.

(1) <u>Administrative Requirements</u>

(a) The State allows a CE for WMM storage.

(b) The WMM are not chemical agents or chemical munitions.

(c) The WMM are stored in accordance with DDESB WMM storage standards and there are no waivers or exemptions to reference (b) for the applicable WMM storage unit.

(d) The installation's Environmental Office notifies the appropriate Federal, State, and/or local environmental regulatory authority of the location of any WMM storage unit within 90 days after the date the unit was first used to store WMM under CE.

(e) The installation ammunition support activity maintains written records of all WMM stored under CE. These records, will be maintained per reference (h), SSIC 8020.1, will contain the following information:

<u>1</u>. The type of WMM stored, by standard nomenclature, lot number, Federal Supply Class (FSC), NSN, DODIC, and Ammunition Condition Code.

<u>2</u>. The quantity of each type of WMM stored.

<u>3</u>. The date that each WMM, by type, was determined to be waste.

<u>4</u>. The last storage date for each WMM, by type.

<u>5</u>. The storage location or locations (e.g., building number or storage pad, and grid coordinates) used to store WMM.

<u>6</u>. The disposition (e.g., destroyed, demilitarized, shipped) and date of action of each WMM, by type.

<u>7</u>. The identity of sending and/or receiving activities/facilities for transported WMM.

(f) At least annually, the ammunition support activity inventories all WMM stored under CE and maintains inventory records for at least three years after the date of each inventory.

(g) At least quarterly, the ammunition support activity inspects WMM stored under CE for compliance with CE storage requirements and maintains records of inspection findings per reference (h) SSIC 8020.1.

(h) All munitions storage units, including those providing CE WMM storage, are subject to installation environmental orders and other SOPs or plans regarding safety, security, and environmental protection. At a minimum, these orders, SOPs, or plans shall, as applicable, establish the installation's minimum munitions storage requirements that include:

<u>1</u>. Maintaining records identifying the type, quantity, and location of munitions stored per references (h) and (i) as applicable.

<u>2</u>. Limiting access to trained and authorized personnel.

<u>3</u>. Establishing procedures for minimizing the possibility of an unpermitted or uncontrolled detonation, release, discharge, or migration of munitions out of any storage

unit when such release, discharge, or migration may endanger human health or the environment.

4. Establishing procedures for ensuring the prompt notification to the installation fire department and Environmental Office in the unlikely event of an unpermitted or uncontrolled detonation or uncontrolled release, discharge, or migration of munitions that may endanger human health or the environment.

(i) Design and Operational Requirements

1. The installation implements procedures to prevent WMM loss or theft.

2. Access to WMM storage is limited to trained and authorized personnel. In this regard, installation personnel and Federal, State, and/or local environmental regulatory personnel briefed on explosives safety are trained and authorized. The ammunition support activity and installation environmental personnel will escort Federal, State, and/or local environmental regulatory personnel during CE WMM storage inspections.

3. The CE WMM storage complies, without a waiver or exemption, with reference (b).

4. The WMM are physically separated (e.g., a separate pallet or shelf) from munitions when both are stored in the same storage unit or area.

5. The WMM are clearly marked and separated for proper identification. (Note: Marking the area [e.g., shelf, pallet, storage facility] where WMM are stored meets this requirement. It is unnecessary to unpack WMM to mark each round or box.)

6. The ammunition support activity manages WMM and WMM residues in accordance with explosives safety and environmental requirements to prevent contaminant migration from CE storage units.

7. For non-chemical agent WMM containing liquids (e.g., munitions with liquid propellants), the CE

storage unit requires secondary containment for promptly detecting and containing liquids or a vapor detection system for promptly detecting liquid vapors. The storage of non-leaking WMM in original shipping or storage containers is secondary containment.

c. Conditional Exemption to Reporting Requirements. The installation Environmental Office will notify its chain of command, DC I&L (LFL), and COMMARCORSYSCOM Code 204 PM Ammo (telephonically or electronically), using the format specified in chapter 13 of reference (b) and, as appropriate, Federal, State, and/or local environmental regulatory authorities (orally) within 24 hours after the installation becomes aware of any WMM loss, theft, CE storage violation, or any unpermitted or uncontrolled WMM detonation, release, discharge, or migration from any storage unit that may endanger human health or the environment. After an oral report to environmental regulatory authority, a follow-up written report describing the applicable circumstances, above, must be submitted within five days after the incident. This reporting requirement is exempt from reports control under paragraph 7.e of reference (ai).

d. Loss of Conditional Exemption. Violations of CE WMM storage requirements may cause the loss of CE. The loss of CE would subject the WMM to full hazardous waste regulations and may result in a regulatory enforcement action.

e. Conditional Exemption Reinstatement. If CE is lost for any WMM in storage, the installation Environmental Office will coordinate with the ammunition support activity to identify the circumstances of the violation and demonstrate that the violation(s) leading to the loss is/are not likely to recur. After this coordination, the installation Environmental Office may apply to regulatory authority for CE reinstatement.

f. Termination of Use and Closure Requirements for Storage Units. Before an installation closes a CE WMM storage unit, it must coordinate the proposed closure with its Environmental Office, COMMARCORSYSCOM Code 204 PM Ammo, and DC I&L (LFL).

14. Return of Reusable Munitions Containers. Except under conditions hindering combat operations, original munitions packaging shall be maintained until all munitions in the packaging are used. Reusable containers shall be returned to

the ASP for disposition. Reference (aj) contains a list of reusable containers for Class V(A) materiel. As conditions warrant, the COMMARCORSYSCOM Code 204 PM Ammo, via AIN, will publish a list of reusable containers for Class V(W) materiel.

15. Ocean Dumping. Absent an emergency, Class V materiel and WMM will not be disposed in national or international waters. Disposition of munitions aboard vessels will follow the Munitions Disposition Process. In an emergency, a ship's CO, after finding that munitions present an immediate danger to the ship or its personnel, may direct munitions overboard to safeguard life at sea.

16. Explosives Safety Submission. Reference (b) requires an Explosives Safety Submission (ESS) and the appropriate site plans to be submitted to DDESB for review and approval to support a munitions response planned for a closed range or real property, other than an operational range, known or suspected of containing Munitions or Explosives of Concern (MEC). Additionally, an ESS after action report is required to be submitted to DDESB following a munitions response for MEC. An ESS will be developed and submitted in accordance with reference (ak).

17. Responsibilities

     a. COMMARCORSYSCOM Responsibilities. COMMARCORSYSCOM shall:

          (1) Designate the Marine Corps DDA for Class V(W) ammunition.

          (2) Coordinate WMM policy, ESS, and after action reports with DC I&L and CG, MCCDC (C465).

          (3) Develop and maintain an ESS repository.

          (4) Prepare guidance for the development of an ESS.

          (5) Review ESS, and any amendments thereto, and forward them to DDESB, as appropriate.

(6) Oversee the explosives safety aspects of munitions response, including ESS implementation, health and safety plan execution, employee qualifications, and quality assurance.

(7) Review and approve after action reports.

b. Class V(W) DDA Responsibilities. In compliance with explosives safety and environmental requirements, the Class V(W) DDA shall:

(1) Designate management of unserviceable Class V(W) munitions and WMM to promote military training and testing while reducing WMM generation.

(2) Designate munitions as WMM.

(3) Coordinate munitions disposition instructions.

(4) Coordinate policy for managing unserviceable munitions and WMM.

(5) Maintain records identifying the type, quantity, and location of munitions stored per references (h) SSIC 8020.1.

c. Ammunition Support Activities Responsibilities. In compliance with explosives safety and environmental requirements, ammunition support activities shall perform the following activities:

(1) Request munitions disposition instructions for unserviceable munitions and WMM.

(2) Execute munitions disposition instructions.

(3) Prepare WMM for shipment.

(4) Complete appropriate shipping control documents if transporting WMM under CE.

(5) Maintain the following records per reference (h) SSIC 8020.1:

(a) Munitions disposition records, including:

<u>1</u>. Munitions disposition requests.

<u>2</u>. Munitions disposition instructions.

(b) ED/CD training records.

(c) Maintain the following records per reference (h) SSIC 8020.1: all shipping documentation for non-waste and WMM transported under CE. For non-waste munitions, maintain copies of shipping control documents per reference (al).

(6) Conduct WMM inspections and inventories, maintain WMM inspections and inventory records, and provide copies of WMM inspection and inventory records to the installation Environmental Office.

d. <u>Installation Environmental Office Responsibilities</u>. The installation Environmental Office shall:

(1) Prepare, sign, and retain copies of HW manifests for off-site WMM transportation not under CE.

(2) Notify regulatory authority in the unlikely event that transported WMM is lost or stolen.

(3) Notify regulatory authority in the event of WMM loss, theft, CE storage violation, or any unpermitted or uncontrolled WMM detonation, release, or migration from any storage unit that may endanger human health or the environment.

(4) Coordinate reinstatement of CE for WMM transportation or storage, if required.

(5) Provide or coordinate hazardous waste training (initial and recurring) for personnel managing or handling WMM.

(6) Audit installation WMM Manager and WMM Handler training records.

(7) Update installation contingency planning to provide for WMM accumulation and/or storage.

(8) Notify COMMARCORSYSCOM Code 204 PM Ammo and DC I&L (LFL), in writing, before closing any operational range.

(9) When applicable, prepare and submit an ESS to COMMARCORSYSCOM Code 204 PM Ammo, via the chain of command, at least 90 days before the planned start of intrusive munitions response activities.

(10) Amend, as appropriate, an approved ESS and submit the amendments to COMMARCORSYSCOM Code 204 PM Ammo, via the chain of command.

18. Deformer Operation

a. Background. Small arms munitions are defined as .50 caliber and smaller. Spent small arms cartridge casing recovery and processing, including mutilation, deforming, or other processing intended to render the expended small arms cartridge casings unusable for their intended purpose, is not considered an explosives operation or hazardous waste treatment.

b. Guidelines. Establishing an installation program to recover, process, and recycle spent small arms cartridge casings is at the sole discretion of each installation's commander. If an installation program is implemented, the following guidelines apply:

(1) A demilitarization operation for processing spent small arms cartridge casings is not considered an explosives operation, provided the following conditions are met:

(a) Spent small arms cartridge casings to be processed by demilitarization (i.e., mutilated or deformed) are first visually or mechanically screened. Screening is intended to ensure that only spent small arms cartridge casings are processed and unused munitions are removed before further processing.

(b) Demilitarization processing equipment is tested to be capable of containing overpressure, fragment, and thermal hazards associated with a worst-case reaction involving a single live round of the most energetic cartridge that could be processed in the equipment. This information can be obtained from the equipment manufacturer.

(c) Demilitarization processing equipment is operated within the manufacturer's specifications and restricted only to the processing of spent small arms cartridge casings.

(d) Demilitarization processing equipment is regularly inspected and maintained to ensure safe operation.

(e) Trained and qualified military or civilian personnel operate the demilitarization equipment.

(2) Demilitarization processing operations meeting the requirements of paragraph 18.b of this chapter and located outside IBD from all PESs do not require submission of a site plan to DDESB.

(3) Locations used for demilitarization processing located within IBD arcs of an explosives site require the submission of a site plan to DDESB, via the chain of command. These locations will be sited at IL Distance or greater, except to the PES to which it is integral.

c. Responsibilities

(1) Installation Commanders. Each installation commander who establishes a program to recover, process, and recycle spent small arms cartridge casings, shall develop installation policy for recovering and processing spent small arms cartridge casings for recycling. They shall also periodically review and update the policy in accordance with this Order, and references (a) and (d).

(2) Organizations Operating Demilitarization Processing Equipment. Organizations recovering, processing, and recycling spent small arms cartridge casings shall:

(a) Ensure that only equipment meeting the requirements of reference (b) is purchased and utilized in demilitarization operations and personnel operating the equipment receive and document their training in its use and maintenance.

(b) Obtain and maintain documentation that the demilitarization equipment has been tested to meet the requirement of containing overpressure, fragment, and thermal hazards associated with an accidental detonation of the most energetic round that could be processed.

(c) Inspect and periodically maintain demilitarization equipment in accordance with the equipment manufacturers' recommendations or standards, and maintain inspection and maintenance records for the life of the equipment.

(d) Prepare SOPs for the operation, inspection, and maintenance of demilitarization equipment in accordance with manufacturers' specifications, this Order, and reference (e).

(e) Establish and maintain records for the final disposition of processed spent small arms cartridge casings. The records should include: locally-developed batch identification numbers for processed scrap metal; the batch weight (in pounds) of processed scrap metal; the name and rank and/or title of the person(s) screening the spent small arms cartridge casing batches; the date(s) the batch screening was performed; by batch, the date of sale or transfer for recycling; and the name of person(s) or organization(s) receiving each batch of processed scrap metal for recycling. Maintain these records per reference (h) SSIC 8015.1.a.

(f) Provide input to the Program Administrator's Report (PAR) (RCS DD-M(A)891), per chapter 2, paragraph G(2) of reference (am).

(3) <u>Installation Explosives Safety Officer</u>. The ESO will:

(a) Periodically review spent small arms cartridge casing screening and demilitarization SOPs.

(b) Periodically inspect small arms cartridge casing screening and demilitarization operations. This may be performed with similar inspections, but will be separately documented.

(c) Periodically inspect the training records for personnel screening spent small arms cartridge casings. Ensure military or DOD civilian personnel performing the screening are listed in the unit commander's appointment list. Ensure contractor operators have documented training. This may be performed with similar inspections, but will be separately documented.

(4) <u>Ammunition Screening Personnel</u>. Personnel screening spent small arms cartridge casings will:

(a) Read and understand spent small arms cartridge casing screening and demilitarization SOPs.

(b) Ensure the accuracy and completeness of their individual training records.

(c) Ensure they are individually appointed, in writing (by the commander for military and DOD civilian personnel, or by senior level supervisor for contractor personnel), to screen spent small arms cartridge casings.

(d) Execute a Free from Explosives Hazard Certification after screening each batch of spent small arms cartridge casings. (The certifications will accompany the screened cartridge casing batches during further processing.)

(e) Return live, misfired, or dud ammunition discovered during spent small arms cartridge casing screening to ammunition storage personnel.

(5) <u>Commanding Officers</u>. COs of organizations processing spent small arms cartridge casings will:

(a) Ensure personnel screening spent small arms cartridge casings are properly trained before assuming their duties.
(b) Ensure the preparation of SOPs for the operation, inspection, and maintenance of demilitarization equipment in accordance with manufacturer specifications, this Order and reference (e).

(c) Individually appoint personnel screening spent small arms cartridge casings to their positions before the personnel perform screening duties.

Chapter 8

Malfunction and Mishap Reporting

1. Background. It is essential to the safety of personnel that all malfunctions, mishaps and accidents involving munitions be immediately reported. Therefore, it is imperative that the provisions outlined in this chapter and all cited references be closely examined and adhered to.

2. Malfunctions. "Malfunction" is the term applied to an explosive material or system when it fails to function in a manner for which it was designed.

3. Responsibilities. Unit commanders are responsible for the following:

   a. Malfunction and Defect Reporting

      (1) Report all malfunctions and defects involving Class V(W) in accordance with reference (an).

      (2) Report all malfunctions involving the use of Class V(A) in accordance with reference (ao).

      (3) An Explosives Mishap Report is an explosive event that meets the requirements of a Class A, B, or C mishap, and will be reported utilizing the Web Enabled Safety System (WESS).

      (4) An Explosives Event Report is an explosive event that does not meet the definition of a Class A, B, or C mishap. Class V(A) incidents are reported in accordance with reference (ao). Class V(W) incidents will be reported in accordance with reference (c).

   b. Maintain a record of all malfunctions and mishaps, including recommendations for preventive measures. Records created in the above paragraphs must be retained and cannot be destroyed.

   c. Notify the installation ESO and provide the ESO copies of any explosives malfunction/mishap reports.

Chapter 9

Explosives Safety Officer (ESO)/Explosives Safety Specialist
Training/Qualification and Certification Requirements

1. Background. In order to conduct an effective explosives safety program, Marine Corps military and civilian ESOs must fully understand not only explosives safety regulatory requirements, but also the interaction between those requirements and the requirements of ammunition life-cycle management. Formal training/experience in a variety of disciplines is necessary to achieve this understanding. Marine Corps ESOs must also have full knowledge of the distinctions among the explosives safety requirements/policies of the various Services in order to function effectively in the increasingly joint operational arena. To this end, COMMARCORSYSCOM, as delegated by CMC SD through reference (ap), is responsible for establishing training/qualification requirements for personnel involved in the conduct of the Marine Corps Class V(W) and non-operational aspects of the Class V(A) Explosives Safety Program. This chapter defines the Marine Corps explosives safety training/qualification requirements. All such requirements are summarized in table 9-1 at the end of this chapter.

2. Letter of Assignment. Installation commanders will appoint, in writing, qualified individuals to serve as ESOs. All Marine Corps installations that routinely store, handle, transport, use, maintain, assemble/disassemble, or train with Class V materials will have an ESO and a formal explosives safety program established. Management and execution of the installation's Explosives Safety Program will be the appointee's primary duty. Due to the multitude of program requirements and specialized knowledge required to perform these duties, all commands should recognize that full-time dedication is essential, and that any additional assignments will be kept to a minimum. Due to the complex issues and catastrophic consequences that may arise, direct access to the installation commander is essential, and the ESO should be a member of the CO's advisory staff. The ESO will be included on all installation facility planning teams/panels/ boards to provide input as necessary.

3. USMC Explosives Safety Officer Certification. A combination of experience and training requirements must be met prior to

COMMARCORSYSCOM Code 204 PM Ammo certifying an ESO. This combination of training and experience is required due to the unique hazards associated with explosives and the multiple disciplines encompassed by explosives safety. The following paragraphs outline the experience and training required to receive initial certification as an ESO and the on-going training required to maintain this certification.

a. Upon completion of both the mandatory training courses and on-the-job training (OJT) (if required), COMMARCORSYSCOM Code 204 PM Ammo will issue a Letter of Certification stating that the individual has met all basic experience and training requirements for certification as a USMC ESO. The certification process should take no more than 24 months to complete. Certification will remain valid for the period stated on the certification.

b. In the event that the size of installation, diversity of mission, operations tempo, or other circumstances dictate the appointment of more than one individual, all general and specific requirements apply to all appointees. ESOs are responsible for establishing and carrying out the installation explosives safety program in accordance with provisions of this publication, and for providing supervision, direction, and guidance to junior personnel.

4. <u>Basic Qualifications</u>. ESOs should be selected from the following listed backgrounds/career fields and have a minimum of four years working experience directly relating to ammunition/ explosives life cycle management:

a. MOSs that directly relate to Class V ammunition/ordnance (e.g., Ammunition Technicians/Specialists/Officers, Aviation Ordnance Men/Officers, Gunner's Mates, EOD personnel, Munitions Technicians).

b. Civilian Safety Specialist (0018) with experience in ammo life cycle management (e.g., storage, transport, maintenance, manufacturing, quality assurance, safety, acquisition).

c. Civilian Quality Assurance Specialist Ammo Surveillance (QASAS) (1910).

d. Civilian Logistics Specialist (0346), with experience in ammo life cycle management (e.g., storage, transport, maintenance, manufacturing, quality assurance, safety, acquisition).

5. Personnel Without Experience

a. Personnel selected as an ESO and not possessing the background and experience will be required to gain this experience under the direct supervision of a certified ESO.

(1) The length of this apprenticeship will be, at minimum, of sufficient duration to encompass one ESSA and one ESI.

(2) Performance of duties, as outlined in this order, and reference (d), during the period of apprenticeship will be assessed by the supervising ESO as "Satisfactory" or "Unsatisfactory." The apprenticeship may be extended until such time as a demonstrated satisfactory rating is attained for all assigned duties/responsibilities.

6. Training

a. All ESOs requiring certification will, within 24 months of appointment meet a minimum level of basic training prior to certification. Course and registration information for web-based training/computer-based training (WBT/CBT) or instructor-led training can be found on the DAC web site (https://www3.dac.army.mil).

b. All initial appointees will complete the following courses:

(1) AMMO-45, Introduction to Ammunition (WBT).

(2) AMMO-76, Identification of Ammunition (WBT).

(3) AMMO-49, Naval Explosives Safety Managers/ Supervisors Orientation (WBT).

(4) AMMO-67, HAZMAT Familiarization and Safety in Transportation (WBT).

(5) AMMO-36, Explosives Safety for Naval Facility Planning (initial course, instructor led).

(6) AMMO-74, Explosives Safety Officer Orientation Course (instructor led). All of the above courses will be completed prior to registering for AMMO-74.

c. Following basic certification, the below courses will be completed within the next 36 months. Initial course will be instructor led; refresher courses may be completed by web based training (WBT).

(1) AMMO-29, Electrical Explosives Safety for Naval Facilities.

(2) AMMO-43, Intermodal Dry Cargo Container/CSC Reinspection.

(3) AMMO-51, Naval Motor Vehicle and Railcar Inspection.

d. Any installation ESO preparing to deploy with a Marine Expeditionary Unit (MEU) or Marine Expeditionary (MEF) will complete AMMO-69 prior to deployment.

e. ESOs, for purposes of continuing training, will complete (at the rate of at least one different course per year) a course selected from the DAC course catalog that is related to explosives safety knowledge or benefits job performance. Ammunition and explosives courses other than those listed in the DAC catalog are acceptable as long as the course pertains to ESO responsibilities and duties. If not in the DAC catalog, a copy of the course description will be sent to COMMARCORSYSCOM Code 204 PM Ammo for evaluation prior to an ESO registering for the course. The following listed courses are recommended examples:

(1) AMMO-5, Ammunition Facilities.

(2) AMMO-10, Ammunition Quality Assurance.

(3) AMMO-20, Chemical Agent Safety.

(4) AMMO-27, Conventional Ammunition Radiation Hazards.

(5) AMMO-60, Technical Ammunition.

(6) AMMO-62, Technical Transportation of Hazardous Materials.

(7) AMMO-63, U.S. Army Explosives Safety (WBT).

(8) AMMO-69, Shipboard Explosives Safety.

(9) AMMO-71, Tools and Equipment.

7. Mandatory Refresher Training. In addition to the above courses the following refresher training will be completed at intervals specified in appendix D of reference (d):

a. AMMO-29, Electrical Explosives Safety for Naval Facilities.

b. AMMO-36, Explosives Safety for Naval Facility Planning.

c. AMMO-43, Intermodal Dry Cargo Container/Convention for Safe Containers Reinspection.

d. AMMO-51, Naval Motor Vehicle and Railcar Inspection.

8. Certification. Certification will only be granted when both course work, and OJT, if required, have been satisfactorily completed. All recommendations for certification will be sent from the base Safety Director to COMMARCORSYSCOM Code 204 PM Ammo.

9. Certification Revocation

a. Certification will be revoked by COMMARCORSYSCOM Code 204 PM Ammo if an individual fails to complete the required refresher training, at COMMARCORSYSCPM Code 204 PM Ammo's discretion. Certification might not be revoked in situations where the individual has explained in writing to COMMARCORSYSCOM Code 204 PM Ammo the circumstances identified and is clearly not responsible for failure to maintain refresher-training requirements. The individual shall make every effort to complete the training requirements. The inability to complete the mandatory continuing training will be reviewed by COMMARCORSYSCOM Code 204 PM Ammo on an annual basis.

b. Certification will be revoked for failure to satisfactorily perform the duties and responsibilities of ESO. In this instance, revocation may be made: (1) by the installation commander or (2) by the ESO's immediate supervisor in consultation and with the concurrence of COMMARCORSYSCOM Code 204 PM Ammo.

c. Certification is mandatory for holding the position of installation ESO. This requirement may be held in abeyance in cases of newly appointed ESO until the new appointee has the opportunity to complete requirements for certification. However, in no case will certification take more than 24 months to complete.

10. Unit/Tenant Explosives Safety Representative

Unit/Tenant commanders will appoint in writing an Explosives Safety Representative (ESR). The ESR will conduct all applicable aspects of the unit explosives safety program and serve as liaison between the unit/tenant and the installation ESO. The installation ESO will advise and monitor these representatives on their conduct of, and compliance with, the explosives safety program. ESRs will require a level of training to competently assist the installation ESO in implementing the installations explosives safety program. ESRs having the training and experience outlined above will not require additional training. ESRs not possessing the experience and training outlined in the above paragraphs will be required to complete the below courses. Upon completion of the below courses, the installation ESO will provide additional OJT in the areas of ESSA, completing Corrective Action Plans, and explosives safety recordkeeping/documentation. ESRs will not receive an ESO certification letter for completing the below courses:

a. AMMO-18, Basics of Naval Explosives Hazard Control.

b. AMMO-45, Introduction to Ammunition.

c. AMMO-76, Identification of Ammunition.

11. Grandfathered Training

All current certified ESOs will be grandfathered into the new certification program requirements. In order to maintain certification, within two years of the date of this Order, all currently certified ESOs will complete any courses listed that were not part of their initial certification. In addition to completing these courses, all current certified ESOs must complete all mandatory refresher training contained in paragraph 7 above.

12. Responsibilities

    a. COMMARCORSYSCOM Code 204 PM Ammo will closely manage and monitor the training and qualification/certification requirements, and perform the following responsibilities:

        (1) Maintain a file of ESOs by name, installation, and training history. This file will be screened annually to determine specific training requirements. This does not relieve individual ESOs of the responsibility for maintaining awareness of their training requirements or shortfalls.

        (2) Contact each ESO individually, and apprise him or her of training requirements and options.

        (3) Review and make recommendations to all training curriculum listed in this chapter, and associated with ESO training.

        (4) Issue a Letter of Certification to USMC ESOs upon completion of the mandatory training courses outlined in this chapter, with a copy to the base Safety Director.

        (5) Issue a Letter of De-Certification to USMC ESOs who fail to maintain currency in training requirements without cause, with a copy to the base Safety Director.

    b. Installation commanders will:

        (1) Appoint, in writing, qualified individuals to serve as ESOs.

(2) Revoke certification of any ESO who fails to satisfactorily perform his or her duties upon concurrence of COMMARCORSYSCOM Code 204 PM Ammo.

c. Installation Safety Directors shall ensure that newly appointed ESOs have completed the requirements for certification within 24 months of assignment.

d. Installation ESOs shall forward copies of all training records and course completion certificates addressed in this chapter to COMMARCORSYSCOM Code 204 PM Ammo via the chain of command.

	Basic Qualification	Experience	On The Job Training (Note 4)	Initial Training (Note 1)	Follow On Training	Continuing Education (Note 2)	Refresher Training (Note 3)
ESO	Civilian Safety Specialist (0018) Civilian Quality Assurance Specialist Ammo Surveillance (QASAS) (1910) Civilian Logistics Specialist (0346) Military Occupational Specialties that directly relate to Class V ammunition/ Ordnance	Minimum 4 years experience directly relating to ammunition/explosives life cycle management.	At a minimum participate in one ESSA and one ESI.	AMMO-36 AMMO-45 AMMO-76 AMMO-49 AMMO-63 AMMO-67 AMMO-74	AMMO-29 AMMO-43 AMMO-51	AMMO-5 AMMO-10 AMMO-20 AMMO-27 AMMO-60 AMMO-62 AMMO-71 AMMO-69	AMMO-29 AMMO-36 AMMO-43 AMMO-51 AMMO-62
ESR	N/A	N/A	N/A	AMMO-18 AMMO-45 AMMO-76	N/A	N/A N/A	

Notes:
1. All courses will be completed prior to registering for AMMO-74.
2. Any ESO who deploy onboard a ship will complete AMMO-69 prior to deployment.
3. Refresher training will be completed at intervals specified in appendix D of reference (d).
4. OJT is only required for personnel not having the basic qualifications and experience identified in chapter 9, paragraph 4. of this Order.

Table 9-1.--Summary of Experience and Training for
Explosives Safety Officer/Explosives Safety Representative

Chapter 10

Installation Explosives Safety Program Requirements

1. Background. Explosives safety is an integral part of each
phase of ammunition life-cycle management. Effective program
management requires that data be collected and analyzed at key
points during this cycle. This data is useful in trend
analysis, allocation of available resources, establishing
resource requirements, identifying/correcting deficiencies,
improving the overall process, and providing management with a
snapshot in time of the effectiveness of the program. Data is
collected and made available to management through a systematic
cycle of inspections, reports, and records. This cycle of
required inspections and reports, and their regulatory basis is
described in this chapter.

2. Inspection Program. Both periodic and random inspections
will be conducted and documented to assess the effectiveness of
the Marine Corps Explosives Safety Program, and monitor status
of individual unit's compliance with Program requirements. The
following are the minimum standards for an installation
explosives safety program. Unless stated otherwise, inspections
are performed and primarily documented by unit personnel. ESOs
are responsible for reviewing all checklists and inspection
documentation, providing follow-up reports as necessary,
training personnel in the use of checklists as necessary, and
ensuring ESO actions are documented for ESI review. All
inspections will be performed utilizing an approved or locally
developed checklist.

   a. Magazine/Storage Facility Inspection. All locations/
facilities used for long or short-term storage or handling of
munitions will be inspected at least annually by the ESO to
ensure compliance with explosives safety standards. For
inspection purposes, the term "magazine" includes all authorized
munitions storage facilities. The inspection shall include an
examination of the facility or location, the surrounding area,
and the material being stored. An SOP written in accordance
with reference (e) shall be developed for this inspection
process. Magazines, magazine areas, and munitions in storage
shall be inspected as described in chapter 11 of reference (d).

(1) Storage inspections are inspections of specific characteristics of ammunition, performed on ammunition in storage; it is not an inspection of the characteristics of storage areas or facilities. Storage inspections verify that ammunition in storage is safe, and is not adversely affected by environmental conditions, handling, or ineffective inventory control.

(a) Storage inspections shall be performed annually (or more frequently, if installation quality history indicates that adverse storage conditions exist) to each ammunition storage area (e.g., magazine, building, warehouse, "shop-store"). These inspections should be performed concurrently with magazine and magazine area inspections and/or local inventory audits/reviews, whenever practical.

(b) An SOP shall be developed and include those requirements appropriate for the storage activity. Storage, magazine, and magazine area inspection requirements may be contained in a single SOP. Storage inspections shall include specific requirements found in chapter 11 of reference (d), and reference (aq).

(2) The ESO shall inspect explosives operating buildings and facilities, to include ammunition handling areas, shipping and receiving facilities, holding yards, maintenance facilities, egresses, and flight equipment shops where munitions operations are regularly conducted. These inspections will be conducted as often as necessary, depending on the hazard associated with the operation, but at least annually. Explosive operating buildings that are being used exclusively for non-explosive operations need not be inspected. If the buildings are to be reused for explosives operations, an inspection will be performed and the site approval reviewed for compliance with proposed operation prior to the start of explosives operations. The pre-operation inspection and site approval review will be documented.

(3) Contingent on available manpower, munitions storage and handling locations with high rates of activity and those located remotely from the main ammunition storage area should be inspected on a more frequent basis, as specified above. The ESO, in conjunction with unit personnel, shall determine the inspection frequency requirements for all locations. Unit personnel may perform these inspections utilizing the required

inspection SOP and checklist. The ESO will review unit-performed inspection documentation on a regular basis and document the review.

(4) The purpose of magazine, magazine area, and storage inspections is to ensure safe storage conditions. ESOs will ensure that organizations responsible for the inspected facilities are informed of all unsafe conditions and that any work orders/repairs that may be necessary are generated by the responsible organization.

(a) A record of work order follow-ups will be maintained and monitored by the ESO.

(b) Any uncompleted work orders, not involving major construction/renovation, in excess of 90 days old will be reported by the ESO, in writing, to the installation commander with copies furnished to the unit commander and to the organization responsible for performing the repair via the installation chain of command. Copies of these reports will be retained by the ESO per reference (h) SSIC 8020.3B for possible review by ESI/DDESB inspection teams. This reporting requirement is exempt from reports control under paragraph 7.h. of reference (ai).

(5) Results will be documented and a summary report generated for the installation commander via the chain of command. Report will include the following elements:

(a) Identify any adverse trends.

(b) Provide recommendations for corrective action.

(c) Identify repeat findings from previous inspection.

(d) List any recommended/required work orders.

(e) List all outstanding/uncompleted work orders.

(f) Note an overall rating for storage facilities (i.e., "Satisfactory" or "Unsatisfactory").

(6) Records of the inspections and actions taken to correct any identified deficiencies should be maintained in the installation Safety Office.

b. <u>Physical/Visual Inspection of Lightning Protection and Electrical Bonding/Grounding Systems</u>. All facilities, locations, and equipment used to store, maintain, handle, or transport munitions will require an inspection of all lightning protection and electrical bonding/grounding systems.

(1) Systems will be tested upon installation. On new primary and secondary ground girdles, measurements of resistance to earth shall be made every month for the first year and at 24-month intervals thereafter, as prescribed by reference (d). Tests will be recorded, and maintained by the installation facilities support organization, and reviewed by the ESO annually. Annual review will be documented by checklist, Memorandum for Record (MRF), or other suitable format. Unit nonconformance to test or record requirements will be reported by the ESO, via letter, to the installation commander with copies furnished to the responsible unit commander.

(2) Visual inspections of lightning protection, grounding systems, and grounded components will be performed at six-month intervals and may be conducted concurrently with magazine inspections and results noted on inspection report or documented separately. Visual inspection criteria may be found in chapters 5, 6, and 8, and appendix F of reference (d). Visual inspection requirements do not apply to permanent aircraft static grounds. Aircraft static grounds shall be tested and marked as required by references (d), (ag), and (ar).

c. <u>Site Inspection</u>

(1) Facilities, such as unit arms rooms, security force armories, storage of inert or display munitions areas, and installation fire departments, shall be inspected at least annually by the ESO. Contingent on available manpower, these locations may be inspected on a more frequent basis.

(2) The ESO, in conjunction with unit personnel, shall determine the inspection frequency requirements for all locations.

(3) Unit personnel may perform more frequent inspections utilizing a locally-approved inspection checklist.

(4) Units will maintain a copy of the inspection checklist per reference (h) SSIC 8000.2a. ESOs will review the unit inspection records, document the review, and make appropriate written report via the chain of command.

    d.   Fire Safety/Fire Protection Equipment Inspection

(1) All locations/facilities involved in the storage, issue/receipt, transport, maintenance, and handling of munitions will conduct regularly scheduled inspections for compliance with fire safety and fire protection equipment requirements. Guidance and inspection criteria may be found in chapter 4 of reference (d). ESOs will monitor units and fire departments to ensure regular inspections are conducted.

(2) This monitoring may be performed in conjunction with other inspections, and will be documented with the inspection checklist or documented separately. Failure of units or fire departments to conduct regular inspections will be reported by the ESO, in writing, to the installation commander with copies furnished to the unit commander and to the organization responsible for performing the inspection. ESOs will maintain a file copy of these reports for a period of three years for ESI/DDESB review purposes.

    e.   Review of Qualification/Certification Program. ESOs will:

(1) Review the installation's Qual/Cert Program.

(2) Meet with representatives of units having personnel in the program, and review records for completeness and accuracy.

(3) Ensure that the annual review by the certifying official is current.

(4) Document reviews by inspection checklist with copies furnished to the unit commander and installation commander.

f. Conduct Annual Explosives Safety Training. ESOs will ensure that annual explosives safety awareness training for all installation personnel involved in the storage, transport, handling, maintenance, receipt/issue, and use of munitions is conducted prior to their assignment to duties involving munitions.

(1) Training will be documented via entries in individual training records.

(2) The course will have a written syllabus. Use of training aids, visual aids, guest expert speakers (e.g., EOD personnel, Fire Chief), and inert display items are encouraged. The following topics are recommended, but not all inclusive, for incorporation into the training syllabus:

(a) Statement/explanation of the explosives safety program goals.

(b) Explanation of HC/D.

(c) SCGs.

(d) Fire/chemical hazard symbols, firefighting procedures, and evacuation distances.

(e) Review of storage, handling, and transport requirements.

(f) Review of sources of information on explosives safety and requirements.

(g) Discussion of SOPs relative to safety warnings, cautions, and equipment.

(h) Discussion of Qual/Cert Program.

(i) Discussion of procedures for handling Materiel Potentially Presenting an Explosive Hazard (MPPEH) or other munitions found on the installation.

g. Explosives Safety Self-Assessment. ESOs will conduct an ESSA on a periodic schedule. The ESSA is a formal program for installations to conduct periodic appraisals of ongoing

munitions operations to determine the effectiveness of their
explosives safety program. ESSAs emphasize the importance of a
proactive approach to explosives safety issues.

(1) The ESSA will be a formal written program. Although
checklist format and content are optional, it is highly
encouraged that ESOs utilize the checklist found in reference
(g) and adapt it to meet installation specific requirements.
The ESSA program will include the following minimum elements:

(a) The installation ESO in conjunction with unit
personnel, will perform periodic reviews of all element of the
munitions mission to address the functional areas, audit
methodology, process quality control, and corrective actions,
and will provide recommendations and solutions to ensure a
comprehensive Explosive Safety Program is achieved. At the
conclusion of the review, a final report of findings and
recommended corrective actions will be prepared by the ESO and
provided to each organization inspected and the installation
commander.

(b) The installation ESO will establish a process to
ensure inspection results are properly analyzed, unfavorable
causes and trends are identified, corrective actions are
accomplished, and controls are implemented to preclude
reoccurrence.

(2) ESSAs may require more time to complete than a
normal ESI, due to such factors as availability of personnel and
mission requirements. Additional guidance on ESSA requirements
is available in Enclosure 4 of reference (g).

3. Files, Records, And Reports

a. Files, records, and reports are as important to a strong
program as good inspections. They document program
effectiveness, and are useful in trend analysis, justification
for manpower and training requirements, as well as tracking
follow-up and long-term corrective actions. Some records are
mandatory, as they directly relate to ESI or other outside
scrutiny. Others, although not mandatory, provide significant
assistance in program management. It is the ESO's
responsibility to establish a means of maintaining associated

documentation that will allow for rapid information retrieval and aid them in program management.

b. The following reports/records and retention intervals are minimum mandatory records to be maintained or accessible to all ESOs. Some records/reports may be maintained by individual units and reviewed by the ESO as part of normally conducted inspections as determined by local conditions or requirements. These reports may be subjected to ESI review. Records created in 3b(1) thru 3b(16) must be retained and can not be destroyed:

(1) Annual Magazine/Storage Facility Inspection Reports. These reports are required for ESI review and contain elements to support other areas, such as SOPs, site plans, and accountability.

(2) Visual Inspections/Tests of Lightning Protection and Electrical Grounding Systems. Visual inspection data shall be stored in a data file for retrieval for use as required for trend analysis or for use by inspection personnel.

(3) Site Inspections. These inspections contain elements for review by ESI, such as storage authorization letters, Qual/Cert review, and SOP review.

(4) Fire Safety/Fire Protection Equipment Inspection Reports. This inspection contains elements subject to ESI review, such as, training, fire drills, response maps, and SOPs.

(5) Hazards of Electromagnetic Radiation to Ordnance Survey. Maintain surveys.

(6) Log of Inert Training/Display Munitions. This log should contain nomenclature of the item, owning organization, location, and certification label number. Maintain perpetually; update quarterly.

(7) DDESB Inspection Reports and Corrective Action Plans. Maintain reports and responses.

(8) ESI Inspection Reports and Corrective Action Plans. Maintain reports and plans.

(9) ESSA Inspections. Maintain ESSA reports.

(10) AMHAZ Board Survey Results. Maintain survey reports and any corrective actions undertaken.

(11) Explosives Safety Site Approvals. Site approvals will be maintained for each facility, as required by reference (d), for as long as the facility is used for storage, handling, manufacture, maintenance, or modification of munitions. Should the facility be removed from service as a munitions site, a site approval request to remove the ESQD arcs must be submitted. This final site approval will be archived, not destroyed.

(12) Commanders' Letters of Storage Authority. Storage authority, as permitted by reference (d) and this Order, that the installation commander has granted will be maintained on file for each facility so authorized.

(13) Inventories of Storage Facilities Constructed prior to May 1967. Reference (d) permits munitions storage in these facilities without explosives safety site approval. It also requires that a written listing of these facilities and details be maintained. This Order requires a more stringent approach mandating that site plans be submitted for all required facilities regardless of construction date. The schedule for submission of these site plans is at the discretion of the installation ESO in coordination with the installation facility planner.

(14) Comprehensive Installation Maps. Comprehensive installation maps, or sets of maps, showing locations and ESQD arcs, storage/operating facilities and locations, explosives vehicle traffic routes, any easements and environmentally sensitive areas, and emergency evacuation routes. Maps will be reviewed annually for correctness and the review documented by an MFR. Both base comprehensive and Fire Department maps will be of sufficient size/scale/clarity, as determined by the user, to be serviceable and useable in daily routine use. Physical areas encompassed by ESQD arcs will be surveyed annually for encroachment by non-ammunition related activities. Any encroachment will be reported to the installation civil engineers, installation commander, and the encroaching organization. All organizations involved will meet within 10 working days to resolve the encroachment problem. Upon resolution, ESOs will submit any necessary changes to the

Explosives Site Plans. Survey will be documented via the same MFR prepared for map review.

       (15) <u>Annual Qualification/Certification Program Review Reports</u>.

       (16) <u>Annual Explosives Safety Training Records</u>. Maintain and update syllabus as required. Maintain record of attendance rosters.

4. <u>Publications and References</u>. Installation ESOs must maintain a current library of reference publications sufficient to conduct research, determine requirements, and provide information upon request. Publications and references may be maintained electronically, provided that personnel can access information when called upon to do so.

    a. These publications will be maintained in an up-to-date status with the latest changes/revisions.

    b. Reviews will be conducted semi-annually to ensure latest changes/revisions have been incorporated.

    c. Records of basic publication or change/revision orders/requests will be maintained until material is received.

    d. Appendix C provides a list of recommended publications.

5. <u>Responsibilities</u>

    a. <u>Installation Commander</u>. Ensure the ESO has direct access to brief issues involving explosives safety or munitions operations.

    b. <u>Installation Safety Director</u>. Ensure that the ESO's primary duty is the management of the installation's explosives safety program. Assigning additional collateral duties to ESOs is highly discouraged; however, should additional duties be assigned, they shall not interfere with the ESO performing his/her primary duty.

    c. <u>Installation ESO</u>

(1) Manage and execute a robust explosives safety program in compliance with this Order and other current regulatory publications.

(2) Conduct/ensure that all required inspections are performed in accordance with this Order and applicable publications, and that the results are properly documented.

(3) Review SOPs, briefs, training plans, and all work requests that relate to explosives safety and munitions operations.

(4) Conduct explosives safety training and briefings, as required or requested.

(5) Ensure that all files, records, and reports are maintained, retained as required, and readily accessible.

(6) Maintain a current publication and reference library of all directives associated with explosives safety and all munitions operations performed aboard the installation. Publications/references may be maintained in paper printed media or electronic media (e.g., CD-ROM, internet).

d. Support Activities. Commanders of activities rendering munitions support are responsible for the following:

(1) Inspect all munitions returned by using units to determine serviceability in accordance with applicable technical manuals.

(2) Request an investigation of munitions reclassified to an unserviceable condition due to misuse. A copy of the request, as well as the results will be provided to COMMARCORSYSCOM Code 204 PM Ammo.

(3) Per chapter 7 of this Order, request munitions disposition instructions for all excess, unserviceable, and obsolete munitions, and WMM.

(4) Ensure the munitions disposition instructions provided by the DDA are implemented as directed.

(5) Ensure all operations involving the storage, handling, transport, security, accountability, management, manufacture, assembly/disassembly, and repair of munitions are conducted in accordance with provisions of this Order and applicable references.

(6) Ensure frequent communications are maintained with installation facilities and environmental offices for awareness of current status.

e. <u>Tenant Unit Commanding Officers and Officers-in-Charge</u>. All tenant unit COs and OICs of unit commands that requisition, receive, handle, store, or transport munitions are responsible for the following:

(1) Designate a responsible ESR to conduct all applicable aspects of the unit's explosives safety program and serve as liaison between the unit/tenant and the installation ESO. The installation ESO will advise and monitor these representatives on their conduct of and compliance with the explosives safety program.

(2) Publish SOPs that govern explosives operations performed within their unit. For those aviation operations for which technical manuals, Naval Air Systems Command (NAVAIRSYSCOM) Conventional Weapons Loading (CWL) manuals and checklists are published, a separate SOP is not required. However, SOPs are required for all common functions, to include storage, handling, transportation, and end-of-life-cycle management. The SOPs shall be prepared in accordance with references (d) and (e), and shall implement the policies and procedures set forth in this Order.

(3) Ensure that all personnel involved in the storage, transport, handling, maintenance, receipt/issue, and use of munitions are qualified and certified, and/or receive explosives safety training prior to their assignment to duties involving munitions.

f. <u>Unit Explosives Safety Representatives</u>. Unit ESRs shall conduct all applicable aspects of the unit's explosives safety program and serve as liaison between the unit and the installation ESO. Unit ESRs will be assigned in writing and are responsible for the following:

(1) Conduct explosives safety training to ensure that all unit personnel involved in the storage, transport, handling, maintenance, receipt/issue, and use of munitions are trained prior to their assignment to duties involving munitions.

(2) Ensure that SOPs governing explosives operations performed within their unit are developed and approved in accordance with references (d) and (e).

(3) Perform required unit inspections, as necessary, utilizing inspection SOPs and approved or installation-developed checklists. Maintain records of completed inspections on file for a period not less than two years from the date of inspection.

(4) Serve as the unit representative to the installation's ESSA program to ensure that inspection results are properly analyzed, unfavorable causes and trends are identified, corrective actions are accomplished, and controls are implemented to preclude recurrence.

Chapter 11

<u>Tactical Explosives Safety for Contingencies, Combat Operations,
Military Operations Other Than War, and Associated Training</u>

1. <u>Background</u>. The Marine Corps continuously trains and
deploys with military munitions. The storage, handling,
transportation, and employment of these items are inherently
hazardous. Full compliance with explosives safety regulations
contained in other chapters of this Order may not be possible
during contingency, combat operations, Military Operations Other
Than War (MOOTW), and associated training. The optional
criteria allowed for in the tactical environment is designed to
provide greater protection (asset preservation distance) for
assets deemed sufficiently critical to warrant the greater
protection, and, in some circumstances, provide lesser
protection (minimum separation distance) for those assets for
which the mission requirements out weigh the increased risk to
those assets. The Marine Corps has had a comprehensive
Explosives Safety Program for many years, with the focus being
geared toward explosives safety in garrison and compliance with
the explosives safety standards of reference (d). Previously,
DDESB allowed DOD components to establish their own explosives
safety programs for the tactical environment. However, with the
addition of chapter 10 to reference (b), DDESB has established
the minimum explosives safety criteria required for the tactical
environment.

2. <u>Tactical Explosives Safety Program</u>. Recently, as a
proactive measure to ensure compliance with DDESB standards,
civilian Tactical Explosives Safety Specialists (TESSs) are
available to provide commanders with tools to compliment force
preservation efforts, and ensure explosives safety during
contingencies, combat operations, MOOTW, and associated
training. The purpose of this program is to support commanders
in protecting forces and assets from potential explosives
incidents that could adversely affect current and future
missions and/or operations within their areas of responsibility
(AORs). The Tactical Explosives Safety Program provides
explosives safety expertise in theater, which is generally not
available to COCOMs during combat and contingency operations.

3. <u>Technical Assistance Visit</u>. The TESS is available to
provide explosives safety support during all combat and training

evolutions. Requests for tactical explosives safety support should be submitted to COMMARCORSYSCOM Code 204 PM Ammo at least 60 days prior to a CONUS operation and 90 days for an Outside Continental United States (OCONUS) operation. Requests should identify the length of time the support is required and the type of support required (e.g., site plans, evaluations, waivers). Further information on the Tactical Explosives Safety Program can be found in reference (ap).

4. <u>Site Plans for Contingency, Combat Operations, and Associated Training</u>. The type of documentation required, and the level at which approval can be granted, will be determined by the operational situation (training or combat) and the type of duration of explosives operations conducted at the site or facility. When the determination is made by the COCOMs or the U.S. Commander of a Joint Task Force (JTF) that the operational tempo will allow for permanent sites, site plans or risk assessments will be submitted for ammunition and explosives storage and operations areas. The types of site plan required and the submission time-frames will be in accordance with chapter 10 of reference (b). Site plan packages will be submitted to the appropriate reviewing authority via the chain of command, in accordance with the site identification (permanent, recurrent, or temporary).

5. <u>Site Approval for Deployed Units</u>. Deployed units will request site approval for all permanent and recurrent explosive sites used to conduct explosives operations. Temporary sites will require a risk assessment. These requests shall be coordinated through the chain of command to COMMARCORSYSCOM Code 204 PM Ammo. During exercises and contingency operations, when prior site approval is not possible, an event waiver is required in accordance with instructions set forth in chapter 1 of this Order.

6. <u>Field Storage</u>. Field storage is primarily intended for situations that require munitions to be stored away from the standard storage environment (e.g., during combat or field training), and is considered temporary in nature. A review and approval of the ammunition storage plan is required from the commander prior to beginning any field/combat operation. Installation commanders may authorize temporary field storage on approved ranges/training areas up to 90 days without prior

approval. The provisions of references (d) and (j) with the
following guidelines will govern temporary storage
facilities/sites:

a. Field storage sites for training operations not located
on approved ranges/training areas shall be formally sited prior
to any explosives operation. The installation commander will
submit a site plan via the chain of submission. Site plans
shall be submitted for all munitions storage or handling
locations, for all vehicle staging areas, and for all secure
explosives holding areas. Once site approval is granted, the
installation commander may authorize and conduct subsequent
temporary field storage at these sites utilizing the ESQD
criteria of reference (d).

b. Reference (j) is for use at advanced bases during
contingency, combat operations, MOOTW, and associated training.
The Field Storage Unit (FSU) concept of this reference may be
used in training provided the location is on an approved
range/training area, or formally sited. However, the ESQD
between PESs and Exposed Sites (ESs) shall not be reduced to
less than the criteria of chapter 7 of reference (d). In
addition, proper SCG integrity shall be maintained at all times
in accordance with chapter 3 of reference (d).

c. For training exercises and activities unable to comply
with the ESQD criteria of reference (d), due to strategic or
other compelling reasons addressing operational necessity,
installation commanders shall request an event waiver prior to
the execution of the explosives operation. Event waivers shall
be prepared and submitted in accordance with chapter 1 of this
Order.

7. Event Waivers. Event waivers for CONUS, OCONUS, and
contingency and combat operations will be submitted as follows:

a. Event waivers for CONUS training operations will be
submitted per chapter 1 of this Order.

b. Event waivers for OCONUS training operations will be
submitted through the chain of command to the operational
commander (e.g., MARFORPAC, COMMARFORCOM, MARCENT) for
operational necessity certification.

c. Risk assessments for explosives operations during contingency and combat operations should be completed per reference (as) and submitted to the applicable commander responsible for the operation.

8. <u>Tactical Safety Specialist Certification</u>. TSSs requiring ESO certification will follow the certification process for an ESO contained in chapter 9 of this Order. Upon completion of the required initial courses and OJT (if required), TSS will have their base Safety Director submit a request for ESO certification to COMMARCORSYSCOM Code 204 PM Ammo. The request will contain all certificates of completion of the required courses and a signed letter stating the TSS has participated in the conduct of an ESSA and an ESI. The request will be endorsed by CMC SD Explosives Safety Branch and forwarded to COMMARCORSYSCOM Code 204 PM Ammo with a recommendation for certification as an ESO. Unacceptable requests will be returned identifying delinquent documentation, course completion. or training. Once certified, the TSS must continue to complete all mandatory refresher training and continual training to maintain certification. The certified TSS will be entered into the ESO Training Database and all training tracked. Any TSS who fails to complete mandatory refresher or continual training will have his or her certification revoked.

Chapter 12

Captured Enemy Ammunition Operations

1. Background. CEA operations pose a significant threat to Operating Forces. There are many unknowns associated with CEA, such as NEW, fuzing mechanisms, markings, and fillers, to name a few. CEA operations are inherently dangerous; thus, the handling, transportation, and destruction of CEA presents a unique challenge for Operating Forces. Leaders at all levels must understand the proper procedures to react to, plan, and execute CEA operations. Operations involving CEA will be assessed using the five-step risk management process to provide maximum protection to personnel and property from an unintentional detonation. CEA operations should ensure that only the minimum number of personnel are exposed to the minimum quantity of CEA for the minimum amount of time.

2. Purpose. The purpose of this chapter is to provide procedural guidance for commanders to safeguard operating forces involved in CEA operations. The major cause of CEA accidents involves untrained personnel handling foreign ordnance. CEA operations include the initial discovery, identification, reporting, handling, transportation, storage, and disposition of CEA. Responsibility during CEA operations involves multiple units. Careful planning, risk management, and the use of trained personnel will help mitigate the hazards of CEA operations.

3. Objective. During contingency operations, Operating Forces have experienced injuries/fatalities involving CEA. CEA operations may necessitate the acceptance of higher risks than would normally be acceptable during other operations. However, when performed by trained and qualified personnel, the handling, transportation, storage, and disposal of CEA can become a safe operation. The objective of this chapter is to:

   a. Establish a baseline policy to be used in any theater.

   b. Establish awareness of the unique hazards associated with CEA.

c. Establish reporting, handling, transportation, security, storage, demilitarization, disposal, and personnel qualifications for CEA operations.

d. Provide guidance for planning and executing CEA operations.

4. Capturing and Reporting Procedures

a. Background. CEA may be encountered during all phases of military operations. Caches of CEA may be as small as one or two pieces of ordnance, or as large as several thousand pieces. Caches can be found in schools, homes, religious sites, hospitals, sewage systems, or in farmers' fields. Large quantities of CEA may also be found in enemy ASPs. Units that discover or capture quantities of stored or cached enemy ammunition and explosives during the course of their operations must ensure that the CEA is properly, safely, and securely handled, transported, or stored as necessary to deny the enemy access to the CEA, and to safeguard personnel and assets.

b. Reporting Procedures. When CEA is encountered during combat operations the senior maneuver commander must determine, based on safety, security, and intelligence considerations, whether the CEA will be destroyed, moved, or held in place. Usually, the combat situation will dictate whether to use, destroy, or secure and retrograde the CEA. Each occurrence should be reported (as found) through command channels as soon the situation allows. The SALUTE (Size, Activity, Location, Unit, Time, and Equipment) report format is recommended when reporting a finding of CEA. FM 21-16, Unexploded Ordnance (UXO) Procedures, may be used to make a tentative identification of the munitions (e.g., projectile, grenade, bomb). The report may be submitted orally or in writing by any means available. This reporting requirement is exempt from reports control under paragraph 7.h of reference (ai). The capturing unit then safeguards the found munitions or continues the mission as directed by higher authority.

c. Capturing Unit. Recovery and evacuation of CEA is a command responsibility. The unit discovering CEA shall immediately secure the site, subject to mission priority, and request qualified personnel inspect the CEA as soon as possible to determine its condition, type, serviceability, hazards, caliber, and SCG. When time and situation permits, sandbag barricades can be built, where practicable and when needed, near, but not touching the CEA to provide fragment protection in the event of accidental detonation prior to arrival of qualified personnel. The capturing unit is responsible for providing security and accountability of the CEA until turned over to another unit, turned in to an established collection point, or turned in to an ASP.

    d. Headquarters Responsibilities. The immediate headquarters of the capturing unit is responsible for:

        (1) Providing prompt disposition instructions.

        (2) Assisting the capturing unit with safeguarding, recovering and evacuating the CEA.

    e. EOD Notification. When notifying EOD of CEA, the commander must provide the following information:

        (1) Grid coordinates.

        (2) Estimated quantity of munitions.

        (3) Initial estimate of the different types of CEA in the cache.

        (4) Whether the site has been secured.

    f. EOD Responsibilities. EOD analyzes and identifies types of munitions in the cache, and determines the following:

        (1) If munitions present a hazard to friendly forces (e.g., booby-trapped or nuclear, biological, chemical [NBC] hazards).

        (2) If the items are safe to handle and/or transport.

    g. Retrograde Operations. If the cache of CEA is to be retrograded, the Combat Logistic Battalion (CLB) will ensure the cache of CEA has been inspected by qualified EOD personnel, and is safe to handle and transport. The CLB will then provide qualified explosives safety personnel, Ammunition Technicians, explosives drivers, and explosives MHE operators to segregate,

and load captured stocks. Transport CEA to the designated
Ammunition Storage Area (ASA). Once CEA arrives at the ASA, it
is stored in a designated secure area within the ASA, but at a
minimum Public Traffic Route Distance (PTRD) from any area
containing U.S. munitions. Regardless of its condition, CEA
shall not be intermingled with U.S. munitions stocks.

    h. Technical Intelligence. EOD will evaluate CEA for
possible Technical Intelligence (TECHINT) exploitation. Initial
reporting of CEA should go through the S-2, and may also be
submitted through EOD channels. If any of the munitions are
identified for technical exploitation, the S-2 will forward a
technical intelligence report to the Assistant Chief of Staff
(Intelligence) (G2/J2). The G2/J2 coordinates evacuation of any
CEA identified for exploitation. Also, civilian or military
ammunition inspectors may assist in inspecting the cache after
EOD has determined there are no extraordinary hazards (e.g.,
booby-traps, time-delay devices, armed munitions). All
hazardous enemy ammunition should be segregated and disposed of
by trained personnel. Any special or unusual characteristics
that may be of interest to TECHINT personnel should be noted and
reported. Reference (at) contains a nine-point format for
reporting UXO that can be adapted and used for reporting CEA.
When units are not sure of the CEA's characteristics, the CEA
should not be moved or destroyed because of unknown hazards
(e.g., toxic and fire hazards associated with liquid propellant,
radiological hazards, hazards associated with chemical or
biological warfare material) may result in a catastrophic
incident.

        (1) Technical Intelligence Reporting Procedures. The
Naval Explosives Ordnance Disposal Technical Center
(NAVEODTECHCEN) will receive notification of all foreign
Explosives Ordnance (EO) items collected. NAVEODTECHCEN shall
be prepared to participate in exploitation of foreign EO items,
or execute the exploitation of such items, upon request of, and
to the extent specifically defined by, the Service having
primary exploitation responsibility. New or unknown items of
foreign EO recovered and rendered safe by EOD personnel,
together with reports relating the circumstances of acquisition,
will be turned over to technical intelligence personnel for
disposition through the appropriate Service's TECHINT channels.
All reports of new and unknown items of foreign EO shall be
transmitted electronically (priority precedence) to the Marine

Corps Detachment (MCD) NAVORDTECHCEN, with information copies to
the CMC (LPE-1) and commanders in the command channel, senior to
the reporting activity. This reporting requirement is exempt
from reports control under paragraph 7.i of reference (ai). The
message shall include, but not limited to:

   (a) Description of the item.

   (b) EOD procedure employed.

   (2) <u>Scientific and Technical Intelligence Reporting</u>.
Copies of all Scientific and Technical (S&T) intelligence
exploitation reports addressing foreign EO shall be forwarded
through Service channels to the appropriate military detachment
at NAVEODTECHCEN, Indian Head, MD, 20640, and/or Naval School,
Explosives Ordnance Disposal (NAVSCOLEOD), Indian Head, MD,
20640. Such reports shall specifically address any "render
safe" or EOD procedures used or developed in the course of
acquiring and exploiting the item. This reporting requirement
is exempt from reports control under paragraph 7.i. S&T
intelligence exploitation report of an EO item should include,
but not necessarily be limited to, the following:

   (a) X-ray print and photographic coverage.

   (b) Complete dimensional data and weight.

   (c) Report of analysis of hazardous components.

   (d) Functioning sequence of fuze and munitions.

   (e) Comparison with similar or like items.

   (f) Reports of any tests performed.

   (g) Chemical analysis of any nonstandard or unusual
materials used in the item.

   i. <u>Captured Material Exploitation Center</u>. The Captured
Material Exploitation Center (CMEC) manages the command
battlefield TECHINT system through the G2/S2. When possible,
other Armed Services should combine assets for the acquisition
and exploitation of CEA. When this occurs, the CMEC becomes the
Joint CMEC (JCMEC).

(1) The CMEC is the first real processor of CEA. When it receives CEA, the CMEC determines its level of TECHINT value. If the item is on the TECHINT requirement list, or it is of TECHINT interest, the CMEC concentrates on exploiting the CEA for immediate tactical or operational use.

(2) The CMEC coordinates evacuation of CEA of special TECHINT interest to and from the CMEC. For items that cannot be evacuated, CMEC organizes and deploys a quick reaction team to coordinate the evacuation of the item or to exploit it on site.

(3) If the item is identified as a first-seen CEA, the TECHINT team, EOD team, or Technical Escort Unit (TEU) forwards a Preliminary Technical Report (PRETECHREP) through command channels to the CMEC. The PRETECHREP gives a general description of the CEA and alerts tactical units to technical information of immediate tactical importance. This reporting requirement is exempt from reports control under paragraph 7.i of reference (ai). Figure 12-1 provides an example of the report format.

(Classification)

PRETECHREP

- **Type of equipment and quantity.**
- **Date and time of capture.**
- **Location (map reference).**
- **Capturing unit and circumstances of capture.**
- **Enemy formation from which captured and origin.**
- **Brief description with serial numbers and, if possible, manufacturer.**
- **Technical characteristics with an immediate value, including information or any photographs available.**
- **Time and origin of message.**
- **Present location of Captured Enemy Equipment (CEE).**

(Classification)

Figure 12-1.--Preliminary Technical Report Format

j. Abandoning CEA. When instructed to abandon CEA, the responsible unit must mark the site. Marking the site alerts other units that the CEA has been found and reported. Marking can be accomplished in a variety of ways. Some of the most common methods of markings are as follows:

(1) Application of engineer tape.

(2) Construction of a small berm around the CEA area.

(3) Surrounding the area with CEE tagged stakes. CEE tags (See figure 12-2) will be placed on stakes near the item, and will be used to describe the CEA. Tags will not be directly attached to the CEA.

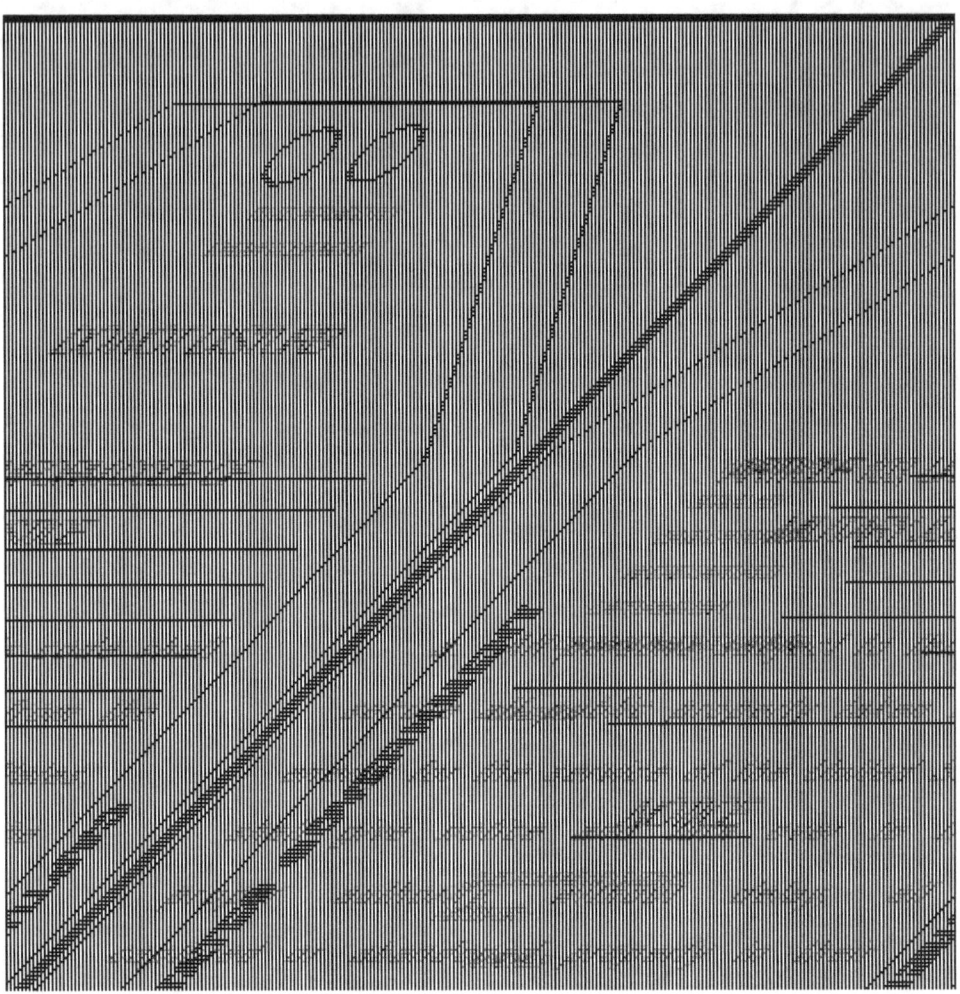

Figure 12-2.-- Sample Captured Enemy Equipment Tag

5. Receipt, Storage, Segregation, and Issue of Captured Enemy Ammunition

    a. Receipt of Captured Enemy Ammunition. CEA must be inspected as soon as possible after receipt to determine its condition, type, and caliber. Only trained and certified EOD personnel shall perform the inspection of all CEA stocks prior to storage. If EOD personnel are unavailable, UXO qualified/certified civilian personnel meeting the requirements listed in DDESB Technical Paper 18 may perform the inspection. However, ASP personnel will identify these stocks as requiring inspection by EOD personnel. Engineers and Ammunition Technicians should not perform inspections on CEA, as they are not trained in the characteristics of foreign munitions. The inspection of CEA shall take place only at designated sites within the storage area. No CEA will be placed into storage without a safety assessment.

    b. Storage of Captured Enemy Ammunition. CEA will be stored in a separate area within the ASA from serviceable and unserviceable DOD munitions. When CEA is placed in storage, protective measures should be taken (e.g., separation distances, use of barricades, fire breaks) to protect DOD serviceable assets. CEA will be stored at a minimum PTRD from DOD munitions. Serviceable and unserviceable CEA should be separated from each other in storage. When space permits, CEA should be stored in multiple small stack quantities. This type of storage is preferred over larger, more volatile stacks.

    c. Captured Enemy Ammunition Storage Compatibility Group. Prior to placing in storage, the CEA should be assessed, if possible to determine its SCG. Qualified explosives personnel (i.e., EOD, UXO qualified civilian personnel) will assess the CEA and determine the SCG. Factors used in determining the CEA SCG are caliber or size, filler, fuzing mechanisms, and NEW. Once SCG is determined, stocks of CEA will be segregated according to the SCG chart located in reference (d).

    d. Determining the Net Explosive Weight of Captured Enemy Ammunition. The NEW of CEA will be calculated using the Service publication on foreign munitions or by using the NEW of a similar type and caliber munitions in the DOD inventory. A non-classified source for NEW foreign ordnance can be obtained from the Naval Ordnance Technical Center, Indian Head, MD. For unknown munitions, the entire weight of munitions will be used as the NEW.

    e. Fire Prevention. The same method used to prevent fires for DOD stocks will be employed in preventing fires for CEA stocks. However, due to the unknown hazard factors associated with CEA, storage areas containing CEA stocks should additionally identify the location of CEA on their fire plan. Fire prevention methods for ASA are located in references (d) and (j).

    f. Serviceable Captured Enemy Ammunition. Serviceable CEA will be retained for security, intelligence, RDT&E, training, demilitarization or other purposes when authorized by the headquarters exercising operational control of the discovering unit's operation. CEA used for any of the above operations shall be clearly marked as "Serviceable." Serviceable CEA shall be segregated from DOD stocks as indicated in paragraph 5b of this chapter.

     g. <u>Unserviceable Captured Enemy Ammunition</u>. Unserviceable CEA stored in the same storage magazine, pad, or container as serviceable CEA will be clearly marked as "Unserviceable," and separated (i.e., sandbagged or placed in other barricaded area). Serviceable and unserviceable CEA will be separated from DOD munitions by PTRD.

     h. <u>Issue of Captured Enemy Ammunition</u>. In unique circumstances, CEA may be issued to using units in the same manner as U.S. munitions. All requests for serviceable CEA are approved and assigned a priority for issue to U.S. units engaged in special missions or training by the COCOM. CEA is issued based on the following priorities:

        (1) Intelligence.

        (2) Special warfare.

        (3) Special Operations Forces.

        (4) Combat units.

        (5) Marine Logistics Group (MLG).

        (6) Substitutes or supplements to U.S. munitions.

    i. <u>Handling</u>

     (1) Trained munitions personnel will supervise the handling of all CEA. No CEA will be handled without certification from EOD that the CEA is safe for movement.

     (2) Handling Exceptions. Engineers trained in the characteristics of CEA may handle CEA without EOD certification in the performance of their duties. Paragraph 8b(2) of this chapter contains the types of CEA engineers who are authorized

to handle CEA without EOD certification. At no time will CEA be moved to an ASP without EOD certification.

   j. Captured Enemy Ammunition Accountability

      (1) CEA that has been inspected, certified, or cleared by EOD or qualified UXO civilian explosives safety inspectors must be receipted, inspected, and accounted for in the same way as DOD munitions. Once CEA is identified as accurately as possible, it is inventoried by the Services for accountability and control. Local stock numbers will be assigned to CEA using the procedures contained in reference (y). Assignment of local stock numbers and accurate accountability should be done as soon as possible after receipt. Reporting and disposition instructions for CEA are the same as for DOD munitions. Close control of CEA is required. CEA can be used as a substitute for bulk explosives during demolition operations.

      (2) CEA shall be accounted for using a method that ensures accountability. A preferred method is using NAVMC 10774 cards; however, spreadsheets, log books, or any means of tracking is acceptable. The preferred method of accounting for CEA is by the piece; however, accounting for CEA by gross weight is also an acceptable method.

6. Transportation

   a. Transporting Captured Enemy Ammunition. CEA should not be transported with DOD ammunition. When possible, CEA should be placed in an unoccupied trailer, and not in the bed of the conveyance. When an armored vehicle is available, it should be used to tow a trailer loaded with CEA to provide additional protection to personnel.

   b. Inspections of Loaded Conveyance

      (1) Inspection at Origin. Before moving or loading CEA into any conveyance, an EOD or TEU team must certify that it is safe to handle and transport. When possible, an ammunition shipping inspector should be consulted about safe loading and tie-down procedures. The EOD or TEU team should provide the driver with any firefighting instructions.

(2) <u>Inspection at Destination</u>. Vehicles loaded with CEA should not be taken directly into the ASP. Vehicles arriving with CEA should be directed to a holding area for inspection by EOD or TEU personnel. Following the transport of CEA, any change noted in the condition of the CEA (e.g., the discovery of a missing safety pin, explosives filler exudation, or other unusual conditions) will be reported to EOD personnel for a new assessment prior to removal from the transport vehicle.

c. <u>Blocking and Bracing</u>. Due to the unknown factors associated with CEA, protection against unintentional detonation associated with the stress of movement is critical. CEA loaded into a conveyance must be secured to prevent movement and its impact with other CEA during transport. Packaged CEA should be secured using cargo straps to prevent movement. Tie down procedures will be followed. Unpackaged CEA should be placed into wooden boxes and then secured to the vehicle. When packaging is not available, the bed of the conveyance can be covered with sand to prevent movement. When using this technique the load should be constantly checked to verify the amount of sand is sufficient to prevent movement and contact with the conveyance. During loading, consideration must be given to protecting exposed fuzes, primers, initiators, and safety devices.

7. <u>Security</u>

a. <u>Responsibility</u>. The senior unit commander is responsible for security of CEA until higher authority provides final disposition.

b. <u>Security in Storage</u>. CEA will be controlled and safeguarded in the same manner as that prescribed for DOD munitions of similar hazard classification, SCG, Security Risk Code (SRC), and caliber and type (e.g., CAT I-like CEA will be handled as CAT I DOD munitions).

8. <u>Demilitarization and Disposal</u>

a. <u>Disposal Operations</u>. Untrained personnel shall not conduct CEA disposal or demilitarization operations. CEA disposal operations conducted by untrained personnel have the potential to cause unnecessary battlefield contamination, personnel injury, collateral damage, and destruction of items required for intelligence. Only authorized personnel will conduct CEA disposal or demilitarization operations. All disposal operations will be conducted in accordance with approved procedures, references (av) and chapter 13 of reference (d).

    b. Authorized Disposal Personnel

        (1) Disposal or demilitarization operations will be performed only by EOD or UXO qualified civilian personnel. Authorizations for disposal operations by combat engineers for limited types and amounts of CEA are contained in paragraph 8b(2) below. EOD, UXO qualified civilian personnel, and combat engineers/engineers will meet the certification and training requirements contained in paragraph 11a of this chapter.

        (2) When EOD or qualified civilian UXO personnel are not available, combat engineers/engineers may dispose of limited types and amounts of CEA. This authorization is granted when the risk of in-action outweighs the risk of immediate action. Destruction of CEA by combat engineers/engineers is limited to only CEA munitions positively identifiable by type, condition, and known hazards. Only CEA munitions 90mm and below and not containing sub-munitions are authorized for destruction by combat engineers/engineers. Authorizing combat engineers/ engineers to dispose of CEA should be limited to the disposal of small cache (e.g., a fighting position with a few unfired mortars, rocket propelled grenades). Large caches of CEA should only be disposed of by trained EOD personnel or UXO qualified civilian personnel.

    c. Donor Material. During planning phases for contingencies operations, theater commanders should develop requirements heavy on basic demolition materials (C4) and initiation systems specifically designed for the destruction of enemy weapons and munitions. The packages should be prepared for multiple transportation modes, and pre-plan the lift requirement into the overall distribution management system. Only serviceable demolition material may be used to support demolition requirements. When disposing of U.S. munitions, CEA may be added in only when additional demolition materials are not required to support the operation.

d. <u>Nuclear, Biological, and Chemical (NBC) Captured Enemy Ammunition (CEA)</u>. A Technical Escort Unit is responsible for securing, transporting, and disposing of NBC CEA after EOD personnel have classified it as safe to handle.

9. <u>Deviations From Standards and Procedures</u>

When the tactical situation dictates deviation from these standards and procedures, the on-scene commander will apply the five step risk management process, and protect personnel and assets to the maximum degree possible.

    a. <u>Risk Assessment Process</u>. The five steps of risk management are as follows:

        (1) Identify hazards.

        (2) Assess hazards to determine risks.

        (3) Develop controls and make risk decisions.

        (4) Implement controls.

        (5) Supervise and evaluate.

    b. <u>Approval Authority for Waivers and Exemptions</u>. The COCOM, U.S. Commander of JTF, Fleet Commander, or DOD COCOM may, for strategic and other compelling reasons, authorize waivers to the explosives safety standards herein for the planning or conduct of CEA operations during contingency, combat operations, and MOOTW. All waivers will be coordinated with the host nation, as required, and consistent with international agreements. Requests for waivers and exemptions to quantity distance (QD) criteria will be per DOD Component directives. When joint operations are being conducted from a single base or location, waivers and exemptions that affect another DOD Component must be coordinated between affected DOD Components. Requests for waivers and exemptions to QD criteria will contain the following:

        (1) A risk analysis for the proposed operation, weighing the need to conduct the operation and violate the standards, against the potential effect of a mishap (e.g., mission impact, loss of resources, turnaround times).

(2) Proposed actions that will eliminate the need for the waiver or exemption. COMMARCORSYSCOM Code 204 PM Ammo will receive copies of all waivers for CEA operations. Waivers for CEA operations during peacetime training will be requested in accordance with references (a) and (d).

10. Explosives Safety Site Planning

a. Separation Distances. CEA will be separated from personnel and assets by distances prescribed in chapter 10 of reference (b) to protect personnel and assets from blast and fragments from an accidental detonation. CEA should be stored in a separate area, isolated by firebreaks, and at PTRD from DOD stocks based on the NEW involved. When PTRD cannot be met, CEA will not be stored any closer than Intermagazine (IM) Distance.

b. Lightning Protection. In the event of a lightning storm, personnel will be evacuated to at least IBD from any area storing CEA. In the event of an explosion, personnel will not re-enter the evacuation zone until EOD personnel have surveyed the area and declared it safe for re-entry.

c. Detonation Sites. Area used for disposing of unserviceable CEA will be placed a minimum of 1,800 feet from stored ammunition and 2,340 feet from all other areas. Sites used for disposing of CEA will be cleared of all vegetation within 500 feet of the detonation point.

d. Site Plan Requirements

(1) Permanent. Locations used for storage or demolition of CEA where operations are expected to exceed 12 months require a DDESB-approved site plan.

(2) Recurrent. Locations used for storage or demolition of CEA where operations are expected to occur on a periodic basis. regardless of the duration of the operation require a DDESB approved site plan or appropriate level of command authorization.

(3) Temporary. Locations used for storage or demolition of CEA where operations are not expected to occur for 12 months and are not expected to occur on a periodic basis require a risk

assessment approved by the applicable commander. The risk assessment will weigh the need for the facility against the potential effects of a mishap.

11. Personnel Qualifications

a. Training Qualifications. Personnel conducting CEA-related operations shall be:

(1) Trained in the characteristics, hazards, and hazard controls of CEA and in safety policy and standards for CEA and CEA operations.

(2) Qualified for the safe conduct of CEA operations.

(3) Briefed on all pertinent procedures for safe handling and/or destruction of CEA, prior to performing CEA operations.

(4) Graduated from the Naval School, Explosive Ordnance Disposal, and meet the training qualifications contained in DDESB TP 18 or, for engineers, have received the Period of Instruction (POI) from EOD on handling, identifying, and disposing of CEA.

b. Authorized Personnel. EOD, UXO civilian qualified personnel, and combat engineers/engineers are authorized to conduct CEA disposal operations. Personnel conducting CEA operations shall be under direct supervision of qualified EOD personnel, unless qualified personnel have determined and documented that risk associated with the CEA operation is acceptable. When EOD is not available, COCOMs (O-5 and above) may authorize combat engineers/engineers to survey and segregate CEA until EOD or UXO civilian personnel become available. Authorization may include destruction of CEA other than the CEA munitions authorized in paragraph 8b(2).

c. Familiarity Training. The world has literally tens of thousands of ordnance items that could be encountered on the modern day battlefield. COCOMs should request familiarity training from EOD about foreign munitions. Familiarity training to theater forces will provide them with specific types and aspects of foreign munitions they may encounter in their areas of operations.

APPENDIX A

GLOSSARY OF TERMS

Ammunition
A contrivance charged with explosives, propellants, pyrotechnics, initiating composition or chemical for use in connection with defense or offense including demolitions, training, ceremonial, or non-operational purposes.

Class V
The military class of supply that consists of ammunition and explosives. Class V(W) is ground ammunition accounted for by COMMARCORSYSCOM Code 204 PM Ammo. Class V(A) is aviation ammunition accounted for by the Naval Ammunition Logistics Center (NALC).

Deviation
A departure from an established explosives safety standard or rule.

Event Waiver
Deviation approved on a case-by-case basis for a particular evolution, issued for a limited period to meet a specific, nonrecurring readiness or operational requirement that cannot otherwise be satisfied.

Exemptions
Deviations from mandatory explosives safety requirements approved for the purpose of long-term satisfaction of recurring readiness or operational requirements.

Explosive Materials
Refers to substances other than soil, such as wood, metal piping, or cloth, that contains sufficient explosive that there is a risk of detonation or deflagration.

Explosives
The term "explosive" or "explosives" includes any chemical compound or mechanical mixture which, when subjected to heat, impact, friction, detonation, or other suitable initiation, undergoes a very rapid chemical change with the evolution of large volumes of highly heated gases which exert pressures in the surrounding medium. The term applies to materials that either detonate or deflagrate.

Explosives
Safety
Submission

A document prepared to ensure that all munitions response actions taken based upon the evaluation of site-specific information fully consider the safe management, handling, storage, transportation, use, and destruction of the munitions that are the objective of the response.

Malfunction

Term applied to an explosive materiel or system when it fails to function in a manner for which it was designed. Malfunctions are categorized as either major or minor.

Military
Munitions
(munitions)

All ammunition products and components produced or used by or for the U.S. DOD or the U.S. Armed Services for national defense and security, including military munitions under the control of the DOD, the U.S. Coast Guard, DOE, and National Guard personnel. The term "military munitions" includes confined gaseous, liquid, and solid propellants; explosives; pyrotechnics; chemical and riot control agents; smokes; and incendiaries used by Components, including bulk explosives and chemical warfare agents, chemical munitions, rockets, guided and ballistic missiles, bombs, warheads, mortar rounds, artillery ammunition, small arms ammunition, grenades, mines, torpedoes, depth charges, cluster munitions and dispensers, demolition charges and devices and components thereof. Military munitions do not include wholly inert items, improvised explosive devices, and nuclear weapons, nuclear devices, and nuclear components thereof. However, the term does include non-nuclear components of nuclear devices, managed under DOE's nuclear program, after all required sanitization operations under the Atomic Energy Act of 1954, as amended, have been completed.

Military Range	A designated land or water area set aside, managed, and used to conduct research on; to develop, test, and evaluate military munitions and explosives, and other ordnance or weapon systems; or to train military personnel in their use and handling. Ranges include firing lines and positions, maneuver areas, firing lanes, test pads, detonation pads, impact areas, and buffer zones with restricted access and exclusion areas. Military ranges also include bodies of water located within the boundaries of a military range (e.g., a stream, lake, pond) or that are themselves a range (e.g., an offshore range in the Atlantic or Pacific ocean). Such water areas include all waters of the United States (as defined under the Clean Water Act) and those ocean waters extending out to 200 nautical miles from the U.S. coast. A military range may be a single site, or may be comprised of several sites.
Misfire	Failure of a component to initiate following an intentional attempt to do so.
Munitions Response	Response actions, including investigation, removal actions, and remedial actions, to address the explosives safety, human health, or environment risks presented by UXO, discarded military munitions (DMM), or Munitions Constituents (MC).
Non-DOD Ammunition	Munitions that are not procured by the DOD and that are not in support of a DOD mission.
Operational Range	A military range that is currently in service and is being regularly used for range activities, or a military range that is not being currently used, but is still considered to be a potential range area, and that has not been put to a new use that is incompatible with range activities.

Real Property	Real estate owned by the United States and under control of the DOD. It includes the land, right title, and interest therein and improvements thereon. Rights and interest include leaseholds, easements, right-of-ways, water rights, air rights, and rights to lateral and sub adjacent support.
Small Arms Ammunition	Ammunition less than or equal to .50 caliber.
Unexploded Ordnance (UXO)	Military munitions that have been primed, fuzed, armed, or otherwise prepared for action, and have been fired, dropped, launched, projected, placed in such a manner as to constitute a hazard to operations, installations, personnel, or material and remain unexploded, either by malfunction, design, or any other cause.
Waiver	Deviation from mandatory explosive safety requirements approved for the purpose of temporary satisfaction of recurring readiness or operational requirements, issued pending the completion of corrective measures to eliminate the need for the waiver.
Waste Military Munitions (WMM)	For purposes of this guidance, a waste military munition is defined as any unused munition that was abandoned by being disposed of, burned, or incinerated, or treated prior to disposal or any used or fired munition that was recovered, collected, and disposed of by burial, land filling, or land treatment. A complete definition can be found in Title 40 CFR Part 266 - Subpart M.

APPENDIX B

ABBREVIATIONS AND ACRONYMS

Acronym	Long Title
AA&E	Arms, Ammunition, and Explosives
AIN	Ammunition Information Notice
AMHAZ	Ammunition and Hazardous Materials
AOA	Aircraft Operating Area
AOR	Area of Responsibility
ASA	Ammunition Storage Area
ASL	Aviation Logistics Support
ASP	Ammunition Supply Point
ASU	Ammunition Storage Unit
AVN	Aviation
CAP	Corrective Action Plan
CBT	Computer-Based Training
CD&I	Combat Development and Integration
CE	Conditional Exemption
CEA	Captured Enemy Ammunition
CFR	Code of Federal Regulations
CG	Commanding General
CLB	Combat Logistic Battalion
CMC	Commandant of the Marine Corps
CMEC	Captured Material Exploitation Center
CNO	Chief of Naval Operations
CO	Commanding Officer
COCOM	Combatant Commander
COMMARCORBASESLANT	Commander Marine Corps Bases Atlantic
COMMARCORBASESPAC	Commander Marine Corps Bases Pacific
COMMARCORSYSCOM	Commander, Marine Corps Systems Command
COMMARFORCOM	Commander, U.S. Marine Forces, Command
COMMARFORPAC	Commander, U.S. Marine Forces, Pacific
COMMARFORRES	Commander, Marine Corps Forces, Reserve
COMNAVAIRSYSCOM	Commander, Naval Air Systems Command
COMNAVSEASYSCOM	Commander, Naval Sea Systems Command
COMNAVSUPSYSCOM	Commander, Naval Supply Systems Command

Acronym	Long Title
CONUS	Continental United States
CWL	Conventional Weapons Loading
DAC	Defense Ammunition Center
DC	Deputy Commandant
DDA	Designated Disposition Authority
DDESB	Department of Defense Explosives Safety Board
DMM	Discarded Military Munitions
DOD	Department of Defense
DODIC	Department of Defense Identification Code
DON	Department of the Navy
DOT	Department of Transportation
DTR	Defense Transportation Regulation
DTS	Defense Transportation System
ECE	Environmental Compliance Evaluation
ED/CD	Emergency Destruct/Combat Disposal
EED	Electro-Explosive Device
EES	Environmental and Explosives Safety
EO	Explosives Ordnance
EOD	Explosive Ordnance Disposal
EPA	Environmental Protection Agency
ES	Exposed Site
ESI	Explosives Safety Inspection
ESO	Explosives Safety Officer
ESQD	Explosives Safety Quantity-Distance
ESR	Explosives Safety Representative
ESS	Explosive Safety Submission
ESSA	Explosives Safety Self-Assessment
ESSO	Explosives Safety Support Office
FARP	Forward Arming and Refueling Point
FBI	Federal Bureau of Investigation
FSC	Federal Supply Class
FSU	Field Storage Unit

Acronym	Long Title
FY	Fiscal Year
HAZMAT	Hazardous Materials
HC/D	Hazard Class/Division
HQMC	Headquarters, U.S. Marine Corps
I&L	Installation and Logistics
IBD	Inhabited Building Distance
IED	Improvised Explosive Devices
IL	Intraline
IM	Inventory Management
ITS	Individual Training Standard
JCMEC	Joint Captured Material Exploitation Center
JTF	Joint Task Force
LFORM	Landing Force Operational Reserve Material
MC	Munitions Constituents
MCBULL	Marine Corps Bulletin
MCCDC	Marine Corps Combat Development Command
MCD	Marine Corps Detachment
MCIEAST	Marine Corps Installations East
MCIWEST	Marine Corps Installations West
MCO	Marine Corps Order
MEC	Munitions or Explosives of Concern
MEF	Marine Expeditionary Force
MEU	Marine Expeditionary Unit
MFR	Memorandum for Record
MHE	Material Handling Equipment
MILCON	Military Construction
MIL-STD	Military Standard
MLA	Mission Load Allowance
MLG	Marine Logistics Group
MOOTW	Military Operations Other Than War
MOS	Military Occupational Specialties

Acronym	Long Title
MPF	Maritime Prepositioning Force
MPPEH	Materiel Potentially Presenting an Explosive Hazard
MPS	Maritime Prepositioning Ship(s)
MR	(Military) Munitions Rule
MWR	Morale, Welfare, and Recreation
NALC	Naval Ammunition Logistics Center
NAR	Notice of Ammunition Reclassification
NATOPS	Naval Aviation Training and Operating Procedures Standardization
NAVAIRSYSCOM	Naval Air Systems Command
NAVEODTECHCEN	Naval Explosives Ordnance Disposal Technical Center
NAVFACENGCOM	Naval Facilities Engineering Command
NAVSCOLEOD	Naval School, Explosives Ordnance Disposal
NAVSEAINST	Naval Sea Systems Command Instruction
NBC	Nuclear, Biological, Chemical
NCIS	Naval Criminal Investigative Service
NEW	Net Explosive Weight
NFEC	Naval Facilities Engineer Command
NSN	National Stock Number
OCONUS	Outside Continental United States
OIC	Officer in Charge
OJT	On-the-Job Training
OPNAVINST	Chief of Naval Operations Instruction
OSHA	Occupational Safety and Health Administration
PES	Potential Explosion Site
PM	Program Manager
PMO	Provost Marshall Office
POI	Period of Instruction
PRETECHREP	Preliminary Technical Report
PTR	Public Traffic Route

Acronym	Long Title
PTRD	Public Traffic Route Distance
QASAS	Quality Assurance Specialist Ammo Surveillance
RBESCT	Risk Based Explosives Safety Criteria Team
RSO	Range Control Officer
RCRA	Resource Conservation and Recovery Act
RDT&E	Research, Development, Test & Evaluation
SAFER	Safety Assessment For Explosives Risk
SALUTE	Size, Activity, Location, Unit, Time, and Equipment
S&T	Scientific and Technical
SAV	Staff Assistance Visit
SCG	Storage Compatibility Group
SD	Safety Division
SECDEF	Secretary of Defense
SECNAV	Secretary of the Navy
SOP	Standard Operating Procedures
SRC	Security Risk Code
TAV	Technical Assistance Visit
TECHINT	Technical Intelligence
TECOM	Training and Education Command
TESS	Tactical Explosives Safety Specialist
UXO	Unexploded Ordnance
WBT	Web-Based Training
WMM	Waste Military Munitions

APPENDIX C

RECOMMENDED PUBLICATIONS

The following is a list of explosives safety publications and instructions recommended to support a sound explosives safety program at Marine Corps installations. This list is not intended to replace the requirement for TMs or MCOs. To obtain the latest series of the listed publications, contact the cognizant releasing authority.

No.	Publication	Title
1	40 CFR	Code of Federal Regulations (CFR), Parts 264 Subpart EE and Part 266 of Subpart M
2	49 CFR	Code of Federal Regulations (CFR), Titles 172, 174, & 177
3	BOE 6000	Bureau of Explosives (BOE) Tariff Service, Hazardous Materials Regulations of the Department of Transportation
4	DOD Regulation P4500.9-R	Defense Transportation Regulation (DTR), Part II, Cargo Movement
5	MCO 1510.78	Individual Training Standards (ITS) System for Ammunition and Explosive Ordnance Disposal Occupational Field, (OCCFLD) 23
6	MCO 3570.1B	Range Safety
7	MCO 3571.2F	Explosive Ordnance Disposal (EOD) Program
8	MCO 4340.1A	Reporting of Missing, Lost, Stolen or Recovered (MLSR) Government Property
9	MCO 5100.29A	Marine Corps Safety Program
10	MCO 8010.1E	Class V(W) Planning Factors for Fleet Marine Force Combat Operations
11	MCO 8023.3A	Personnel Qualification and Certification Program for Class V Ammunition and Explosives
12	MCO 8025.1D	Class V(W) Malfunction and Defect Reporting
13	MCO P4030.19H	Preparing Hazardous Materials for Military Air Shipments

No.	Publication	Title
14	MCO P4400.150E	Consumer Level Supply Policy Manual
15	MCO P5090.2A	Environmental Compliance and Protection Manual
16	OPNAVINST 5102.1D /MCO P5102.1B	Navy and Marine Corps Mishap and Safety Investigation, Reporting, and Record Keeping Manual
17	NAVAIR 00-80T-103	NATOPS Conventional Weapons Handling Procedures Manual (ASHORE)
18	NAVFAC P-300	Management of Civil Engineering Support Equipment
19	NAVFAC P-307	Management of Weight Handling Equipment
20	NAVFACINST 11010.45	Regional Planning Instruction Overview
21	NAVSEA OP 2173 Vol 1 & 2	Approved Handling Equipment for Weapons and Explosives
22	NAVSEA OP 3565 Vol 1	Electromagnetic Radiation Hazards
23	NAVSEA OP 3565 Vol 2 Pt 1	Electromagnetic Radiation Hazards
24	NAVSEA OP 3565 Vol 2 Pt 2	Electromagnetic Radiation Hazards
25	NAVSEA OP 4	Ammunition and Explosives Safety Afloat
26	NAVSEA OP 5 Vol 1	Ammunition and Explosives Ashore Safety Regulations for Handling, Storage, Production, Renovation and Shipping
27	NAVSEA OP 5 Vol 3	Ammunition and Explosives Ashore Safety Regulations for Handling, Storage, Production, Renovation and Shipping
28	NAVSEA SG420-AP-MMA-010	Periodic Testing Arrangements for Ordnance Handling Equipment
29	NAVSEA SW010-AF-ORD-010	Identification of Ammunition
30	NAVSEA SW020-AC-SAF-010	Transportation and Storage Data for Ammunition, Explosives and Related Hazardous Material

No.	Publication	Title
31	NAVSEA SW020-AF-ABK-010	Motor Vehicle Driver & Shipping Inspector's Manual for Ammunition, Explosives, and Related Hazardous Materials
32	NAVSEA SW020-AG-SAF-010	Navy Transportation Safety Handbook for Ammunition, Explosives and Related Hazardous Materials
33	NAVSEA SW023-AG-WHM-010	On-Station Movement of Ammunition and Explosives by Truck and Railcar
34	NAVSEA SW023-AH-WHM-010	Handling, Ammunition, and Explosives with Industrial Materials Handling Equipment (MHE)
35	NOSSAINST 8020.14	Shore Station Explosives Safety Inspections
36	NOSSAINST 8023.11	Standard Operating Procedures for the Processing of Expendable Ordnance at Navy and Marine Activities
37	NAVSEAINST 8020.6D	Navy Weapon System Safety Program
38	NAVSEAINST 8020.7C	Hazards of Electromagnetic Radiation to Ordnance Safety Program
39	NAVSEAINST 8020.9A	Ammunition and Explosives Personnel Qualification and Certification Program
40	NAVSEAINST 8020.18A	Ammo & Explosives Driver 12-Hour Training Course/Self Assessment Transportation Guide
41	NAVSUP Manual, Volume V	Naval Supply Systems Command Manual, Volume V, Transportation of Property
42	NAVSUP Pub 538	Management of Materials Handling Equipment (MHE) and Shipboard Mobile Support Equipment (SMSE)
43	NAVSUP P-724	Conventional Ordnance Stockpile Management
44	NAVSUP PUB P-805	Ammunition Sentencing (Receipt, Storage and Issue; Cognizant Segregation; Fleet Sentencing; Visual Aids), Vol 1
45	NAVSUP PUB	Conventional Ammunition Sentencing - Fleet Sentencing, Vol 3

No.	Publication	Title
	P-807	
46	OPNAVINST 5530.13C	Department of the Navy Physical Security Instruction for Conventional Arms, Ammunition, and Explosives (AA&E)
47	OPNAVINST 5530.14D	Navy Physical Security
48	OPNAVINST 5585.2	Military Working Dog Manual
49	OPNAVINST 8020.14/ MCO P8020.11	Department of the Navy Explosives Safety Policy
50	OPNAVINST 8000.16B	Naval Ordnance Maintenance Management Program (NOMMP)
51	SECNAVINST 8020.3C	Responsibilities for Issuance and Administration of Waivers and Exemptions from Department of Defense (DOD) Explosives Safety Standards
52	UM4400-124	SASSY Users Manual
53	UM4400-15	Organic Procedures for Supply
54	DODI 2030.08	Trade Security Controls on DOD Excess and Surplus Personal Property
55	DOD 4160.21-M	Defense Materiel Disposition Manual
56	DOD 4160.21-M-1	Defense Demilitarization Manual
57	DOD Instruction 4140.62	Management and Disposition of Material Potentially Presenting an Explosive Hazard (MPPEH)

APPENDIX D

INDEX